UNFORCED RHYTHMS

of Grace

Dr. Lynn Hiles

UNFORCED RHYTHMS

of Grace

- The grace of God that flows from rest -

Lynn Hiles Ministries
P.O. Box 127
Great Cacapon, WV 25422

This book and all other books and materials by Dr. Lynn Hiles are available at www.lynnhiles.com or by phone at 304-579-5336.

For Worldwide Distribution
Printed in the U.S.A.

ISBN 978-0-9839034-0-6

First Printing: 2011

DEDICATION

I would first like to dedicate this to my incredible wife Joyce who is the most important person in my life other than the Holy Spirit. It takes an incredibly special woman to be married to a man who travels the nations of the earth carrying a message of love and hope and unselfishly shares me with the world. She works tirelessly behind the scenes in so many unnoticed roles to support and help fulfill the vision that God has given us both. She is truly the unsung hero and deserves more credit than do I. Without her there would be no Lynn Hiles Ministries. She unselfishly has remained at home running my office and raising our two wonderful sons Jeremy and Jason, who have grown to be incredible men of God. They are my credentials. To me success is not measured by how many people know my name or how many books I write or television programs I appear on. Success is a family passionately in love with Jesus; a demonstration that the real gospel really works. This includes not only my two sons. It includes their wives as well. Liza is married to Jeremy and Becky is married to Jason. Jeremy has grown up to be an incredible preacher in his own right and is now following in my footsteps. I highly recommend him. Jason is the executive producer of our weekly television program and my personal assistant who travels with me. He is an awesome musician, speaker and worshiper. Last, but not least, I dedicate this to my first grandbaby Ellen Grace who has her grandpa wrapped around her little finger. It is for future generations and my children's children and for your children that I do what I do.

Contents

PREFACE

The quest for truth is like an exciting treasure hunt. The more we search the unsearchable riches of Christ, the more we discover it is multilayered. For those who are satisfied with the surface truths of the historical, grammatical, literal fulfillment of Scriptures, we make no argument. We believe those truths are in fact there. To the hungry heart that has a desire to go deeper and plumb the depths of the unsearchable riches of Christ, this book is written. Truth is like an onion. The more you peel it, the more layers you discover. In the following pages we are not trying to do away with the natural interpretation of these miracles. They in fact took place, and from that we can glean Jesus is still a miracle worker. However, if all of the things that Jesus did were written in the books as Scripture says, I reckon that the books could not contain it. So consider with me the possibility that the miracles recorded in the Scriptures may have been hand-picked by the Holy Spirit to show us a deeper and more profound meaning if we can unravel its typology. Come with me on this incredible treasure hunt and perhaps at the end you will be enriched by the mining of this vein of truth. Open your mind to the teacher called the Holy Spirit who can open to you the mother-load of revelation that flows from God's greatest treasure, which is a revelation of Jesus Christ, His person and His work.

FOREWORD

My first exposure to Dr. Lynn Hiles was in 1997, as I listened to a set of his tapes someone gave me. I was immediately captivated and liberated by the power of his words. My first thoughts were, "Never has such a man spoken!" At that moment, my life became a mutual demolition and construction site as the winds of change began to blow.

Dr. Hiles is one of the great voices of reformation and affirmation in the earth today. His messages are releasing the grace of God that will tear down old mindsets and simultaneously establish the mind of Christ. In this book, Dr. Hiles articulates the finished work of Christ in such a way readers can expect the winds of change to begin to blow in their life. Many are searching for such a change. It is the change that brings the peace and rest that Jesus provided in His redemptive work. Without that change, we risk continuing to live irrelevant, worn out, confused lives that are ineffective. This book is essential to the maturing of the body of Christ.

In Revelation 18:21 the word of God declares...And a mighty angel took a stone like a great millstone, and cast it into the sea, saying, Thus with violence shall that great city Babylon be thrown down, and shall be found no more at all.

As you read the words of this book, Dr. Hiles becomes such a messenger. This book becomes a great millstone breaking the power of religious confusion; a confusion that has burdened the people of God, making their lives irrelevant and ineffective. It is time to quit living our lives without the rest and peace Jesus provided for us! Get ready to experience the liberating power of the finished work of Jesus, as you enter into His Sabbath Day.

Pastor Justin Phillips
Lake City Christian Fellowship

INTRODUCTION

A careful study of Hebrews 4 will cause the reader to conclude that the promised land is more than just a piece of real estate. It is faith in Christ and His finished work that brings us into this incredible promise land called rest. Christ is the fulfillment of all the promises that God made to the fathers. In Christ all of God's promises are yes and amen. It is from the posture of rest that there is a steady outflow of milk and honey. Rest does not mean that we become spiritual couch potatoes. It simply means that everything that flows from our lives is a result of Him working in me and living His life through me. I am utterly dependent upon Him. Without Him I can do nothing. But with Him I can do all things. A land that flows with milk and honey is the abundant life at every level. It is the good life physically and spiritually. "Moses my servant is dead" are the words that fall from the lips of our heavenly Father as He introduces us to Joshua. Moses symbolizes the sweat and labor of human effort trying to work in order to receive God's favor through old covenant performance. A greater than Moses is now on the scene. Our heavenly Joshua, Jesus Christ, is leading us into a promised land called rest.

The only requirement for entering into this rest is faith. When we truly believe and trust Him we will rest. When we rest God will work, and when we work God will rest. Life will become a whole lot easier when we learn to trust the One who has never failed. In Hebrews 4 they did not enter in because of unbelief, although the works were finished from the foundation of the world. It is the revelation of the finished work that produces faith. The only requirement of the new covenant is that you believe. Everything that you do from there on is a result of what you believe. Right living flows out of right believing.

> *"Let us labour therefore to enter into that rest, lest any man fall after the same example of unbelief."* (Heb. 4:11 KJV)

At first glance it almost looks like this scripture is contradicting everything I just said. However compare that to this scripture:

> *"Jesus answered and said unto them, This is the work of God, that ye believe on him whom he hath sent."* (John 6:29 KJV)

This verse clearly tells us that the work of God is simply to believe. The only fight in the New Testament is the fight of faith. When we believe and trust in Christ and His finished work we will truly enter His rest.

Some of our critics have accused us of giving people a license to sin; to which I reply that they have been sinning without a license for years. Grace does not give people license to sin, it empowers them not to. The grace of God teaches us to deny ungodliness. Let's take a look at this scripture:

> *"For the word of God is living and active and sharper than any two-edged sword, and piercing as far as the division of soul and spirit, of both joints and marrow, and able to judge the thoughts and intentions of the heart. And there is no creature hidden from His sight, but all things are open and laid bare to the eyes of Him with whom we have to do. Therefore, since we have a great high priest who has passed through the heavens, Jesus the Son of God, let us hold fast our confession. For we do not have a high priest who cannot sympathize with our weaknesses, but One who has been tempted in all things as we are,*

yet without sin. Therefore let us draw near with confidence to the throne of grace, so that we may receive mercy and find grace to help in time of need." (Heb. 4:12-16 NASU)

In these verses it is not just any word that is life-giving and powerful. It is the word that flows from the rest. Remember the context here is rest. The word that flows from the rest will reveal what is in a man's heart. As you read the words of this book what is really in your heart will begin to surface. If you read the words of this book and your conclusion is, "I am free to sin". Please do not blame the message. What the message did was reveal what was already in your heart. You are naked and open before the eyes of Him with whom we have to do. I am not suggesting that you act on what you have discovered is in your heart. I am admonishing you and imploring you to come boldly to the throne of grace and receive mercy. It is there that you will find grace to help in the time of need. It is in this environment of grace and rest that you will find a faithful High Priest who has been tempted in every temptation known to man, yet without sin. And because He now lives inside of us He is able to conquer every giant that is in our land. Get ready because you are about to live in houses you did not build and eat from the fruit of vineyards you did not plant. You are about to enter into another man's work, the work of Jesus Christ.

Do not listen to the 10 spies who always point out the giants and the walls and how big the enemy is and all the reasons why you cannot live in this Promised Land. Hear the words of this writer declaring we are well able to take the land. We are more than conquerors through Him that loved us and gave himself for us. My focus is not on the size of the giants but on how big God is. My focus is on the size of the fruit in this land. There are grapes here the size of pumpkins. It takes more than one person to carry them. Won't you join me in this Promised Land called rest and together, corporately, we can carry forth the fruit of this land where we become a land that flows with milk and honey.

Chapter One

UNFORCED RHYTHMS OF GRACE

"Come unto me all you who are weary and heavy laden and I will give you rest" ring the resounding words of our Savior as He addresses a crowd of tired and weary people, who by now, were completely worn out with a works-based religious system. These refreshing words still breathe hope and life into the weary soul of many in this hour. I am afraid that in many religious circles people walk down a church aisle and trade one set of stress and problems for another. They have not found relief from their burdens and in many cases, leave with more piled on than with which they came. They were offered a religion rather than a relationship, fear instead of faith, law instead of love.

I can remember a story of a man who walked a church aisle to give his heart to the Lord. Before he could even really pray through, he was ushered away into a Sunday school room where well-meaning people were collecting his address and trying to sign him up for all kinds of classes and church activities. His response to them was, "I didn't want to buy a timeshare. I wanted to give my heart to the Lord." While I do believe it is important to get people involved, sometimes I think we are so zealous for new membership that we worry about that more than we worry about the person having a real encounter with the Lord. I am afraid that many people did not come to know Jesus at all in a personal way; they bought a fire insurance policy. People fill church pews every Sunday morning to keep the fire insurance policy current. Folk don't know if they love God or not, they just know they don't like the alternative. Fear has been the motivation. They were invited to a last day barbecue and were the object that was on it. While I do believe that it is important that we warn men to flee from the wrath to come, I also believe that, in the words of the apostle Paul in Romans 2:4, "...it is the goodness of God that leads men to repentance." I truly believe that if we would preach the grace and goodness of God, men would run *from* sin and run *to* God. One of the great deceptions is we think sin is the source of our pleasure; and God is the source of our pain, when in fact it is the exact opposite. As a result we run *from* God and run *to* sin thinking it will bring pleasure, when in reality all it does is bring more misery. If we can only renew our minds to the truth that sin is always the source of pain and God is always the source of pleasure, people would run *from* sin and run *to* God every time! The result of this erroneous thinking has left multitudes of casualties. I am convinced that many, who no longer attend church and think that they have rejected God, have really not rejected Him at all. They have rejected religion and they should. Religion has piled up so many requirements with all its various hang-ups, with all of its dress codes and sin conscious preaching and performance-based ideas. Most of this is unscriptural and folks finally just got so weary and worn out they threw in the towel and quit. It reminds me of an old commercial where a young boy was riding his bicycle up a hill. He was peddling his bicycle for all he was worth. Someone said, "This boy is running out of steam and he needs some cereal." I was once that boy growing up in classical Pentecost trying to peddle my spiritual bicycle up all of the religious hills of man-made rules, trying to please a God that I could never quite please. I can remember going to revival as a young man and sitting under what I call terrorist preachers, who must have had a fight with their wife on the way to church just to get their game face on. They looked angry and perhaps they were. Religion has a way of doing that to you. It leaves you frustrated and disappointed. They would pull their glasses down on their nose and pull their pants about midway up their chest, and lean back and say, "You want me to name sin? I'll name it for you tonight!" They would proceed to preach against everything that you can imagine including devil's food cake and deviled eggs just because it had the word "devil" in it; but you could eat angel food cake. You could not drink Coca-Cola for two reasons. Because you drink it from a bottle and other beverages such as beer are also in a bottle, you must shun the appearance of evil. Also, because it was shaped like a woman, it might cause you to lust. How ridiculous! If you are struggling with a Coca-Cola bottle, buy a three liter bottle and get over it. It was a sin to take physical education when I was in high school because you had to wear shorts to participate, and that wasn't holy. It was a sin to play baseball. The general rule here was that if it was fun, it had to be sin. What a thief religion is! It will take your life. When in fact Jesus says, "I came that you might have life and that more abundantly." The abundant life can only flow from rest. I used to get saved about every revival and sometimes between revivals. I would ask God to kill me at the altar because I knew I couldn't make it until next week having to keep all these rules. According to them I had lost my salvation. They were offering me eternal life that in most cases only lasted a couple of hours. This boy was running out of steam and needed some spiritual cereal. If you have reached that point in your walk with God, this book is for you! If you are tired of pedaling uphill and your Christian walk has not been a joy, but a struggle, and you never feel like you are quite good enough to find the favor of God, then let me point you in the direction of the One who will help you find rest for your soul. Please notice the context of the Scripture before Jesus offers a much needed rest.

> *"But whereunto shall I liken this generation? It is like unto children sitting in the markets, and calling unto their fellows, And saying, We have piped unto you, and ye have not danced; we have mourned unto you, and ye have not lamented. For John came neither eating nor drinking, and they say, He hath a devil. The Son of man came eating and drinking, and they say, Behold a man gluttonous, and a winebibber, a friend of publicans and sinners. But wisdom is justified of her children."* (Matt. 11:16-19 KJV).

You did not dance to our music! You are not meeting our criteria! But look at what Jesus has to say about it.

> *"Come unto me, all ye that labour and are heavy laden, and I will give you rest. Take my yoke upon you, and learn of me; for I am meek and lowly in heart: and ye shall find rest unto your souls. For my yoke is easy, and my burden is light."* (Matt. 11:28-30 KJV)

It is even clearer when we read from The Message Bible. Let's take a look.

> *"Are you tired? Worn out? Burned out on religion? Come to me. Get away with me and you'll recover your life. I'll show you how to take a real rest. Walk with me and work with me — watch how I do it. Learn the unforced rhythms of grace. I won't lay anything heavy or ill-fitting on you. Keep company with me and you'll learn to live freely and lightly."* (Matt. 11:28-30 MSG)

Does that describe you? Are you tired, worn-out, burned out on religion? If so, it's time for a get-away for some much needed rest. Let us learn the unforced rhythms of grace! It is time to disconnect yourself from the religious yoke of bondage and take His yoke upon you; and this time instead of learning about religion we will learn about Him. What we will learn about Him will bring us into an incredible rest. We will study the person and work of Christ and as we do you will see how the work truly got finished. It is one thing to tell people to rest. It is another thing to show them how the work got finished so they can truly rest. It is much like telling someone who knows that the lawn needs to be mowed, to rest. You might even convince them to sit down on a chair and act like they are resting, but in the back of their mind they know that sooner or later the lawn has to be mowed. On the other hand, if you take them out and show them someone has already mowed the lawn for them, they can truly come in and rest knowing the work is finished. That's what the preaching of the cross does for the believer. It shows them how the work got finished. I think it is important to note that much of Jesus' preaching about rest was not to sinners on the street but to people who had been under the bondage of religion most of their lives. He was about to bring them into a perpetual Sabbath day; a rest that still remained for the children of God. Let's look at the purpose of Sabbath.

> *"But the seventh day is the sabbath of the LORD thy God: in it thou shalt not do any work, thou, nor thy son, nor thy daughter, nor thy manservant, nor thy maidservant, nor thine ox, nor thine ass, nor any of thy cattle, nor thy stranger that is within thy gates; that thy manservant and thy maidservant may rest as well as thou. **And remember** that thou wast a servant in the land of Egypt, and that the LORD thy God brought thee out thence through a mighty hand and by a stretched out arm: therefore the LORD thy God commanded thee to keep the sabbath day."* (Deut. 5:14-15 KJV)

SERVANTS OR SONS

The purpose of the Sabbath was to remember first of all that you were a servant. In the old covenant you were a servant. In the new covenant you're a son.

> *"Wherefore thou art no more a servant, but a son; and if a son, then an heir of God through Christ."* (Gal. 4:7 KJV)

> *"For as many as are led by the Spirit of God, they are the sons of God. For ye have not received the spirit of bondage again to fear; but ye have received the Spirit of adoption, whereby we cry, Abba, Father."* (Rom. 8:14-16 KJV)

> *"SEE WHAT [an incredible] quality of love the Father has given (shown, bestowed on) us, that we should [be permitted*

to] be named and called and counted the children of God! And so we are! The reason that the world does not know (recognize, acknowledge) us is that it does not know (recognize, acknowledge) Him." (1 John 3:1 AMP)

One of the great truths in the New Testament is that we are no longer servants, but sons. What an incredible quality of love the father has bestowed upon us. He has sent the Spirit of His Son into our hearts crying Abba. We have not received the spirit of bondage that operates through fear. We are not under the slave masters of Egypt. We have been delivered by the blood of the spotless Lamb! We are not simply serving God. We are now heirs of God. We have his DNA, his Divine Nature Attributes. We now have a life and not a law. Jesus arrived on the scene to set us free from the tyranny of having to serve because of fear of retribution. This time He was delivering them not from a physical bondage, but from a spiritual bondage called religion and its taskmaster of fear. The Sabbath was meant to remember how He brought us out. How did He bring us out? He brought us out by the blood of the spotless Lamb. The work is truly finished. We have come to a perpetual rest because we dwell in Him who completely finished the work. My Sabbath day is more than a day of the week. It is a person! His name is Jesus.

Let us examine a little bit closer what this slave master really is.

> *"Even so we, when we were children, were in bondage under the elements of the world: But when the fulness of the time was come, God sent forth his Son, made of a woman, made under the law, To redeem them that were under the law, that we might receive the adoption of sons. And because ye are sons, God hath sent forth the Spirit of his Son into your hearts, crying, Abba, Father. Wherefore thou art no more a servant, but a son; and if a son, then an heir of God through Christ." (Gal. 4:3-7 KJV)*

In this text it is clear we were in bondage to the law. We did not just need redemption from sin. We needed redemption from the law. It's what we were in bondage to. It operated through fear of death (Heb. 2:15). I am convinced it is much easier to get people delivered from sin than it is to get them delivered from religion. Above in Romans 8:14 it tells us that those that "are led by the Spirit of God, they are the sons of God." The contrast in this verse is to look at what you were being led by before. The answer is you were being led by rules and regulations from an old covenant. Now you're not being led by an external set of rules, but by an internal indwelling Spirit of God. His Spirit does not lead you into lawlessness. It leads you to the law of the Spirit of life in Christ Jesus. There is a new governor living inside of you called the Spirit of God. You have become the governor's mansion. The apostle Paul once said "the love of Christ constrains me". Love is much more powerful than law. Faith is much more motivating than fear. Relationship works far greater than rules. It is out of our relationship and learning from Him that He teaches us the unforced rhythms of grace. Someone might say, "That sounds like greasy grace to me", to which I reply by paraphrasing the words of Titus, it is the grace of God that teaches us to deny ungodliness. Grace is a teacher.

> *"For the **grace of God** that bringeth salvation hath appeared to all men, **Teaching us that, denying ungodliness** and worldly lusts, we should live soberly, righteously, and godly, in this present world;"* (Titus 2:11-12 KJV)

The Tree of the Knowledge of Good and Evil

Please don't misunderstand me. I am not suggesting that you get free from the law so that you can come into bondage to sin. For whom the Son sets free is free indeed. I don't want you to be in bondage to either sin or religion, because one is just as bad as the other. You see, in an ancient garden six millenniums ago God told the first man Adam he could eat from all of the trees that are in the garden except the tree of the knowledge of good and evil.

"For in the day that you eat you will surely die" Genesis 2:17. Please notice He did not say to him if you eat the good that is on this tree and leave the evil alone you will be okay. That is what is taught over pulpits every week in churches. Eat the good and stay away from the evil, not realizing the good will kill you just as quickly as the evil, only it is more deceptive.

> *"There is a way which seemeth right unto a man, but the end thereof are the ways of death."* (Prov. 14:12 KJV)

You see, there is a way that seems right to a man. This verse did not say there is a way that seems wrong to a man. The end is still death because it is the tree of the knowledge of good and evil. There is a completely different tree that we must feed from. That tree stands on Mount Calvary. When I feed from what this tree produced, this tree gives me life. You see, we ate our way into this problem; now we must eat our way out of the problem. We must change our spiritual eating habits. We must feed on the finished work of the cross, on the person and work of Jesus Christ and what He redeemed us from. He did not just redeem us from sin. He also redeemed us from the curse of the law.

> *"Christ hath redeemed us from the curse of the law, being made a curse for us: for it is written, Cursed is every one that hangeth on a tree:"* (Gal. 3:13 KJV)

He saved us not just from sin but from the wrath of God.

> *"Much more then, being now justified by his blood, we shall be saved from wrath through him."* (Rom. 5:9 KJV)

God offered us a new diet in the New Testament. Remember, Jesus was laid in a manger and a manger is a feeding trough. It is where we should be bringing our flocks to feed. We should feed them on Christ and Christ alone. Certainly, without question, He delivers us from the bondage of sin. That goes without saying. The gospel of grace does not suggest that God does not want to change us. What is in question is how He does that. You see, He doesn't want you to be in bondage to anything; to sin or religion. His desire for us is to be transformed and not conformed.

Conformed or Transformed

> *"And be not conformed to this world: but be ye transformed by the renewing of your mind, that ye may prove what is that good, and acceptable, and perfect, will of God."* (Rom. 12:2 KJV)

What is the difference you might ask? When the apostle Paul was talking about being conformed to this world, he was talking about an age. The Greek word for world in this text is age. The age that he was talking about was the age of the law. That age with its whole cosmetic message of conformity was rapidly coming to an end. A new messianic age of transformation was now on the horizon. Let's look at it in a different translation.

> *"I therefore beg of you, please, brethren, through the instrumentality of the aforementioned mercies of God, by a once-for-all presentation to place your bodies at the disposal of God, a sacrifice, a living one, a holy one, well-pleasing, your rational, sacred service, [rational, in that this service is performed by the exercise of the mind]. And stop assuming an outward expression that does not come from within you and is not representative of what you are in your inner being but is patterned after this age; but change your outward expression to one that comes from within and is representative of your inner being, by the renewing of your mind, resulting in your putting to the test what is the will of God, the good and well-pleasing and complete will, and having found that it meets specifications, place your approval upon it."* (Rom. 12:1-2 WUEST)

The concept of conformity is to take an external set of rules and regulations and impose them on people to make them change. It is not something that is truly in their hearts. The concept of transformation is to change from the inside out, much like the change of the caterpillar and butterfly are through metamorphosis. As a matter of fact, the Greek word for "transformation" is where we derive the English word metamorphosis. The caterpillar does not wait for something outside of itself to change, because built into its DNA is everything it needs to become a butterfly. Much like the butterfly, everything we need to become the sons of God is written into our spiritual DNA at the moment of our new birth. That's what the cocoon of grace does for us. It wraps us in God's unconditional love that begins to change our hearts. It is not a behavior modification or self-help program. It is a divine influence upon our hearts with its reflection in our lives. If our hearts are truly changed, then our behavior will reflect it. What religion does is change behavior. What grace does is change hearts. The old covenant was written to the old man to try to get Adam to behave. The new covenant is written to the new man to develop and mature the new creation. What we must stop doing in our ministries is preaching to old Adam and begin to feed and minister to the new man a steady diet of who he is in Christ until faith arises in his heart and he begins to act out of what he now believes is true of him. Right believing will produce right living. Our problem is we are constantly telling people what is wrong with them and preaching against everything instead of preaching for something. When I was growing up someone would ask us, "What do you believe?" My response would always be that we don't believe women should cut their hair. We don't believe you should wear shorts. We don't believe women should wear pant suits. We don't believe you should watch television. I would always tell them what we didn't believe. Because the truth was I had sat in church most of my life and didn't believe in much of anything. I had sat right in church and became an unbeliever because no one ever preached anything I could believe in. It was always about what we didn't believe. Of course that's what the book of Galatians said the law does, it shuts up faith.

> "And the law is not of faith: but, The man that doeth them shall live in them." (Gal. 3:12 KJV)

"But before faith came, we were kept under the law, shut up unto the faith which should afterwards be revealed." (Gal. 3:23 KJV)

I wonder what would happen if we spent as much time telling people who they are in Christ instead of what is wrong with them. If we put our emphasis on developing the new creature as much as we have in beating up the old one, we would be much further ahead. If we could simply preach what Christ did for us and as us, if we would preach Him and not us, we might become what I call believers. We must give people something to believe. The real gospel does this. It makes a believer out of you. When you become a believer you will act out of what you truly believe. If you believe you are the righteousness of God you will act like you are righteous. "For the just shall live by faith..." (Gal. 3:11). Right believing really does produce right living. What really needs changing is our belief system.

Many years ago the Lord began to deal with me about my philosophy of ministry. I was on an airplane to Florida and the Lord began to rebuke me from the book of Ephesians. Here's what He said.

ALL THINGS UNTO EDIFICATION

"Let no corrupt communication proceed out of your mouth, but that which is good to the use of edifying, that it may minister grace unto the hearers. And grieve not the holy Spirit of God, whereby ye are sealed unto the day of redemption. Let all bitterness, and wrath, and anger, and clamour, and evil speaking, be put away from you, with all malice: And be ye kind one to another, tenderhearted, forgiving one another, even as God for Christ's sake hath forgiven you." (Eph. 4:29-32 KJV)

When the Father said this to me, my response was, "Lord, what is corrupt communication? Am I saying curse words that you don't approve of?" (Thinking that perhaps I had picked up some street slang or something that maybe God was not pleased with; I began to search my heart.) The Father said to me, "Son, I'm not talking about what you call curse words, but I am in fact dealing with you about cursing." I then began to realize that what He was saying was every time you preach the law, you are putting people back under the curse and you are cursing them. You are setting them up for failure.

> *"For as many as are of the works of the law are under the curse: for it is written, Cursed is every one that continueth not in all things which are written in the book of the law to do them. But that no man is justified by the law in the sight of God, it is evident: for, The just shall live by faith. And the law is not of faith: but, The man that doeth them shall live in them. Christ hath redeemed us from the curse of the law, being made a curse for us: for it is written, Cursed is every one that hangeth on a tree:"* (Gal. 3:10-13 KJV)

It is no wonder we have such discouragement in the body of Christ today. We preach the parts of the law that fit our culture and we call that the gospel. Every time we step into the pulpit we disqualify the people of God and wonder why they don't draw near with a true heart in full assurance of faith. We tell them God is angry with them. We tell them all the things that are wrong with them and we tell them why God can't bless them. We browbeat them with our rules, regulations and human ideas. We shut up their faith and then wonder why we don't see miracles. Let me say, that is corrupt communication and it is grieving the Holy Spirit of God! It is a worse kind of cursing than using street slang. Let me simply say that if you are preaching Adam and who we are in him, you are preaching the wrong man. But if you preach Christ and Him crucified, and how that affected us, you are preaching the right man. It is the difference between saying something to a child like, "You little brat. You will never amount to anything." or saying to him, "You are too good of a child to act like that. That is not who you are." Both are correcting him, but one edifies him and gives him faith in which to operate, while the other belittles and humiliates and discourages him. It is detrimental and it does not minister grace to the hearer. Our prisons are full of people who have been told all their lives that they will never amount to anything. They mixed the word that we spoke over them with faith and believed exactly what we said. Then we are surprised when they end up failures. The Father then said this to me:

> "Study to shew thyself approved unto God, a workman that needeth not to be ashamed, rightly dividing the word of truth." (2 Tim. 2:15 KJV)

I used to think this scripture meant that if I would study enough maybe someday God would use me. And yes, it does mean we need to study. But it is what we need to study that was revealed to me. I need to study to show myself approved unto God. What I used to do was study what was wrong with me, and instead of receiving God's approval, I always felt disapproved. Rightly dividing the word of truth in this text does not simply mean we must learn to study Greek and Hebrew. It means we must be able to divide what is truth in relationship to the old covenant and what is truth in relationship to the new covenant. The old covenant disapproves you and disqualifies you. The new covenant shows you how you got approved and accepted in the beloved. It was through the person and work of Jesus Christ and His finished work. When Paul wrote to Philemon, this is what he said.

> "That the communication of thy faith may become effectual by the acknowledging of every good thing which is in you in Christ Jesus." (Philem. 6 KJV)

We communicate our faith by acknowledging every good thing that is in you, not by pointing out everything that is wrong with you. When we preach the law it shuts up faith. The whole purpose of the law was to conclude that all are under sin so that He could have mercy on all (Rom. 3:9-31 and Gal. 3:22). It was designed to bring you to Christ. After you have worn yourself out on the religious treadmill of works and sweat, somewhere you will run out of steam. It is at that point that you will look up and say, "I need a Savior", because you just can't do this. That's what the law was designed to do. Moses, the mediator of that covenant, did not make it into the Promised Land by the works of the law. That used to frustrate me because I thought if Moses couldn't make it, and he was the mediator of that covenant, then I didn't have a chance. I used to think God was being unfair because Moses only messed up one time and missed the Promised Land. Of course, under the old covenant if you are guilty of one sin, you are guilty of all. But then I realized that if Moses would have made it, you and I would have been forever destined to enter in by the works of the law rather than by the hearing of faith. Moses, who is a type of the law, could not bring them into the Promised Land. Only Joshua whose name is the Old Testament Hebrew word Yeshua; the new covenant name Jesus, could bring them into a true rest. In the book of Joshua, God makes this announcement, "Moses my servant is dead. Now therefore arise, go over this Jordan, thou and this entire people, unto the land which I do give to them, even to the children of Israel." In the new covenant, the Promised Land is not a piece of real estate. It is a person. When we get in Him there is an outflow of milk and honey. Jesus Christ, our heavenly Joshua, is the fulfillment of all the promises that God made to the fathers. In Christ all of God's promises are yes and amen. He is our Promised Land! He is our inheritance! What a glorious inheritance it is. When you are in Him you have truly found the place of rest. Hebrews 4 talks about rest. Please read the whole chapter. It says they did not enter in because of unbelief. They did not mix the word with faith when the gospel was preached to them. The apostle admonishes us not to fall after the same example of unbelief. It tells us in verse three that we, which have believed, do enter into rest. Your question might be, believed what? The answer is the gospel.

The Gospel is the Power of God unto Salvation

"For unto us was the gospel preached, as well as unto them: but the word preached did not profit them, not being mixed with faith in them that heard it." (Heb. 4:2 KJV)

The apostle Paul calls the gospel the preaching of the grace of Christ. The word "gospel" means the good news. It is the preaching of the person and work of Jesus Christ. That brings us into this grace.

> *"I marvel that ye are so soon removed from him that called*
> *you into the grace of Christ unto another gospel: Which is not*
> *another; but there be some that trouble you, and would pervert*
> *the gospel of Christ."* (Gal. 1:6-7 KJV)

The response could possibly be "when was the gospel preached to them?" The answer is it was preached to them in types and shadows all through the wilderness journey. When a spotless lamb was taken out from among the sheep and goats and the blood was applied to the door posts, the gospel was preached. When the Red Sea was opened and they were buried in baptism, the gospel was preached. When the rock was smitten in the wilderness and water came out, the gospel was preached. Was it not a picture of the smiting of the rock Christ Jesus? He was the rock that followed them. When the manna fell and the children of Israel were fed by the manna, was that not a picture of the true Bread that came down from heaven, even Christ (Jn. 6:32)? When the serpent was lifted up on a pole, was that not a picture of the lifting up of Jesus to the cross to spoil principalities and powers (Jn. 3:14)? Exactly 50 days after the Passover lamb had been slain in Egypt they came to Sinai where the law was given and 3,000 people dropped dead. Could we not compare that to the New Testament where 50 days after Jesus, the true Lamb was slain, there were followers in an upper room awaiting the promise of the Spirit and another cloud came down and 3,000 people were added to the church? I don't think it's an accident that the number 3,000 is used in both cases. In the old covenant, when the law was given the letter killed. In the New Testament, when the Spirit was given 50 days after Passover, God, by His Spirit, wrote His law on our hearts and the Spirit made us alive. As a matter of fact, all of the stopping stations of the wilderness journey had something to do with the person and work of Jesus Christ. No matter what you have been in bondage to, whether it is sin or religion, there is nothing that you have been bound by that the revelation of the finished work of the cross cannot deliver you from. Oh yes, the gospel was certainly preached to the children of Israel. They may not have understood it, but it was preached every morning when they would get up and there was manna. Every time water flowed from the smitten rock, the gospel was preached. I am convinced that the preaching of the cross is the power of God unto salvation. The preaching of the cross and the finished work of Christ is the vehicle that will bring you into rest. Israel's problem was unbelief. The only real requirement of the New Testament is that you believe. Everything else flows out of what we believe. If we have a flawed belief system we will fall after the same example of unbelief as did the children of Israel in the wilderness journey (Heb.4:11). If we will simply believe the gospel of Christ it will bring us into a perpetual rest. It will bring us into a glorious Promise Land called Christ; not to become spiritual couch potatoes where we do nothing, but into a land called Christ where there is an outflow of milk and honey. It is a place where the fruit of the Spirit is so abundant, that much like Joshua and Caleb it takes more than one person to carry it. It is simply living out of the overflow of the work of Christ and allowing Him to live His life through us.

> *"And I have given you a land for which ye did not labour, and cities which ye built not, and ye dwell in them; of the vineyards and oliveyards which ye planted not do ye eat."* (Josh. 24:13 KJV)

You see, true rest does not come by ignoring the work. It comes by understanding how the work got finished. That is what the preaching of the cross does. It shows you how the work got finished. It brings you into a perpetual Sabbath day. To me, honoring the Sabbath day, to keep it holy, simply means that what Jesus did was enough. I will not dishonor the Sabbath day by trying to do all over what Jesus has already done. I am not looking for a law I can keep, I am looking for a life that can keep me. Jesus is my Sabbath.

*"So don't let anyone condemn you for what you eat or drink, or for not celebrating certain holy days or new moon ceremonies or Sabbaths. For these rules are only shadows of the reality yet to come. **And Christ himself is that reality.**"* (Col. 2:16-18 NLT)

"The Spirit of the Lord is upon me, because he hath anointed me to preach the gospel to the poor; he hath sent me to heal the brokenhearted, to preach deliverance to the captives, and recovering of sight to the blind, to set at liberty them that are bruised, To preach the acceptable year of the Lord. And he closed the book, and he gave it again to the minister, and sat down. And the eyes of all them that were in the synagogue were fastened on him. And he began to say unto them, This day is this scripture fulfilled in your ears." (Luke 4:18-21 KJV)

I think ample proof has been made through the scriptures that the Sabbath day in the New Testament is more than just a certain day. My point is not to discuss which day we should worship. I will leave that to your personal conviction.

"One man esteemeth one day above another: another esteemeth every day alike. Let every man be fully persuaded in his own mind. He that regardeth the day, regardeth it unto the Lord; and he that regardeth not the day, to the Lord he doth not regard it. He that eateth, eateth to the Lord, for he giveth God thanks; and he that eateth not, to the Lord he eateth not, and giveth God thanks." (Rom. 14:5-6 KJV)

My goal is to simply point out that the Sabbath day was made for the man and not the man for the Sabbath. The Sabbath was to give us rest from our sweat and labor. Remember that in the garden of Gethsemane Jesus prayed until He sweated great drops of blood. When the blood that flowed from the

Divine Brow touched a cursed Earth, it redeemed us from an ancient curse in a long-ago garden that said we will earn our bread by the sweat of our brow "until" you return to the ground. You see, when you were buried with Him, you returned to the ground, but now you've been raised, free from the curse with the resurrection life pulsating in your being. I think it is important to note the venue that Jesus was in when He preached this message. He was not talking to drug dealers on the streets or prostitutes or what we call sinners. He was talking to people who had been in church all their lives. He was sent to the brokenhearted. Who could you find that was more brokenhearted than people who had turned to what they thought was God and all they got was religion? They are disappointed and broken. He was sent to the captives. Who do you know that needs to be set free from captivity more than people who are in religious bondage? He was sent to remove blindness and to touch those who are bruised. I believe there are those who are bruised and have been wounded by well-meaning, works-based religious ideas that have made them spiritually blind. The poor are not just people who do not have any money; they are the poor in spirit who are in a real spiritual deficit. They desperately need the gospel, the good news. If the gospel is ever preached to the poor they will not be poor anymore. If the brokenhearted ever hear the good news their hearts will heal. If the captive hear the sound of the Jubilee trumpet they will drop whatever they are in bondage to and go back and take their inheritance! Jesus, in this text, announces the acceptable year of the Lord, the year of the favor of our God, or more literally, the year of Jubilee.

The year of Jubilee was the year of favor. It came every 50 years or after seven Sabbaths of years. It was a compound of Sabbaths. It was given so that the Israelite could not lose his inheritance forever (Lev.25). Please read the whole chapter. It was given to restore. On the Jubilee a long loud blast from a ram's horn proclaimed liberty throughout the land. The ram's horn came from the death of a male lamb. The true male Lamb was now standing in their midst and He had come to set the captive free. He was the ultimate Jubilee, and He was now standing in their synagogue. He put the trumpet to His lips and announced "this day is this scripture fulfilled in your ears." Be encouraged, because we stand in Christ. We stand on favored ground. It is a perpetual day of favor and grace. We have now come to the ultimate of Sabbath days, the ultimate Jubilee. The moment you hear the ram's horn ringing in your ears you can drop whatever you have been in bondage to, whether it is religion or sin. You have been set free from your slavery in order to possess your inheritance to regain your family and to be restored to your rightful place. That is what the Sabbath is for. In the coming chapters we will examine the miracles that Jesus did on the Sabbath day, and we will show you how they are a picture of what flows from this incredible rest.

Chapter Two

CORN ON THE SABBATH

"Verily I say unto you, Among them that are born of women there hath not risen a greater than John the Baptist: notwithstanding he that is least in the kingdom of heaven is greater than he. And from the days of John the Baptist until now the kingdom of heaven suffereth violence, and the violent take it by force. For all the prophets and the law prophesied until John. And if ye will receive it, this is Elias, which was for to come." (Matt. 11:11-14 KJV)

John the Baptist was, according to the words of Jesus, one of the greatest men ever born of women. However, John the Baptist was the last of the old covenant prophets. His prophetic ministry was announcing the imminent availability of the Kingdom of God. It was now at hand. The King of the kingdom was now walking planet Earth and was about to be introduced by John at the Jordan River. I do not think it is an accident that John the Baptist saw the Spirit of God descending from heaven like a dove. You see, when Noah built his ark, God was giving him a vehicle out of an old world dominated by sin and the curse, and it would bring him to rest on a mountain called Ararat. The word Ararat means the curse is reversed.[1] As the ark was emerging from the flood, an old world was being washed away by water. A new world where the curse had been reversed was about to come into view. Noah released two birds from the ark. One of them was an unclean bird, and it flew all the way through the scriptures and landed in the book of Revelation where Babylon has become a hold of every foul spirit and the cage of every unclean and hateful bird. But the dove only had to fly to the book of Matthew where he finds Jesus, the true ark emerging from the waters of baptism. When the dove, which is a symbol of the Holy Spirit, landed on Jesus he had just found the New World where the curse was reversed. He landed on the olive branch which symbolizes a covenant of peace. The rainbow of God's new covenant would rest in the person and work of Jesus Christ. Emerging from the muddy waters of the Jordan River was the king of all kings who would open a door into the everlasting Kingdom of God through the new birth experience. The blood, the water and the Spirit were now the medium by which we enter the Kingdom of God. No longer would man have to take the Kingdom of God by force. He would simply just have to receive it as a free gift.

In this new covenant, it is the Father's good pleasure to give you the kingdom. It is no longer earned, but freely given. You see all the law and the prophets prophesied until John. Until is a time word that culminated with John. Anyone who has been born again has entered the kingdom by virtue of his or her new birth. That person now has the indwelling Spirit of God. No one in the old covenant had this abiding presence. So he that is least in the kingdom of heaven is greater than any of the old covenant Prophets. They did not have eternal life living in their spirits. They were not born again. They had not been translated out of the kingdom of darkness and into the kingdom of His dear Son. Let's look at it from The Message Bible.

> *"For a long time now people have tried to force themselves into God's kingdom. But if you read the books of the Prophets and God's Law closely, you will see them culminate in John, teaming up with him in preparing the way for the Messiah of the kingdom."* (Matt. 11:12-13 MSG)

You see, the kingdom replaced the law. A brand new covenant was about to be given. The new covenant is the constitution of the kingdom. A new form of governing God's people was coming on the scene. No longer would an external code written on tablets of stone govern us, but an internal, indwelling Holy Spirit would now be the moral compass of our lives. We were about to become the governor's mansion. The abundance of grace and the gift of righteousness was about to empower us to reign in life by one Christ Jesus (Romans 5:17). From this time forward everything would flow from this incredible rest. This time we were in this Ark called Christ. We were baptized into Christ. We left the old world and now the abiding presence of the Holy Spirit dove abides with us forever. Right now we are citizens of the Kingdom of God with access to all the kingdom has to offer. This time we do not have to violently take it. We simply flow out of rest, out of the finished work, out of the perpetual Sabbath; it is the unforced rhythm of grace. It is not by works lest any man should boast. Let's take a look at some of the activities that Jesus did on the Sabbath.

> "At that time Jesus went on the sabbath day through the corn; and his disciples were an hungred, and began to pluck the ears of corn, and to eat. But when the Pharisees saw it, they said unto him, Behold, thy disciples do that which is not lawful to do upon the sabbath day. But he said unto them, Have ye not read what David did, when he was an hungred, and they that were with him; How he entered into the house of God, and did eat the shewbread, which was not lawful for him to eat, neither for them which were with him, but only for the priests? Or have ye not read in the law, how that on the sabbath days the priests in the temple profane the sabbath, and are blameless? But I say unto you, That in this place is one greater than the temple. But if ye had known what this meaneth, I will have mercy, and not sacrifice, ye would not have condemned the guiltless. For the Son of man is Lord even of the sabbath day." (Matt. 12:1-8 KJV)

Except a Corn of Wheat

To fully understand this miracle we must first take a look at the symbolism of corn. Let me say first of all that by no means am I taking away from historic literal fulfillment of the Scripture. Jesus really walked through a cornfield and picked corn over 2000 years ago. However, any spiritually minded Bible student can certainly see in story after story that, often times, there are much deeper and hidden truths to be discovered by understanding the types and shadows. There are prophetic pictures that, like a grand tapestry, unfold the unsearchable riches of redemption's story. The things that Jesus did on the Sabbath day give us a glorious picture of what flows from rest. Rest flows from the finished work of Christ.

> *"Verily, verily, I say unto you, Except a corn of wheat fall into the ground and die, it abideth alone: but if it die, it bringeth forth much fruit."* (John 12:24 KJV)

It is incredible to me that the very first miracle that Jesus does on the Sabbath day holds the basic key to understanding the rest of the miracles. All of it has to flow from what He has accomplished in His death, burial, and resurrection, for it is truly what has produced our rest. This Scripture is clearly dealing with His sacrificial death. First of all, because it pictures the truth that He is hungry to feed on what His death has produced, I believe there is expectancy in the heart of Jesus to truly reap what He has sown. In this perpetual Sabbath day, He is truly hungry to find a whole field full of ripe corn that are the results of what He planted in His death, burial and resurrection. We are truly His harvest. In the Old Testament during the time of the first fruit the people would take a sheath of wheat or corn and wave it before the Lord as a wave offering. That wave offering was symbolizing that there is a harvest to follow. Christ was the incorruptible seed that fell to the earth and died, and we are the product of that seed. We have the same nature and characteristics as the original seed, except multiplied many times over.

"Let him that is taught in the word communicate unto him that teacheth in all good things. Be not deceived; God is not mocked: for whatsoever a man soweth, that shall he also reap. For he that soweth to his flesh shall of the flesh reap corruption; but he that soweth to the Spirit shall of the Spirit reap life everlasting. And let us not be weary in well doing: for in due season we shall reap, if we faint not." (Gal. 6:6-9 KJV)

Any time I have ever heard this scripture preached it was used to terrify me. It was always used to modify someone's behavior. And while I do believe in the principle of sowing and reaping, the truth is we have not always reaped everything we have ever sown. Thank God for that!

The first application of this scripture is really dealing with the giving of finances to those who communicate to us in the word. In that context, sowing to the flesh literally means to be giving finances to those who preach the law. And sowing to the spirit means to be giving your finances to those who preach the gospel of grace and the new covenant. It is the difference between Levi which represents the old covenant priesthood, who has a commandment to take tithes of the people, and the new covenant priesthood of Melchizedek, who brings forth bread and wine; which symbolizes the new covenant as he received tithes of the people. One takes and the other receives. One is law and the other is grace. One is flesh and the other is Spirit. We are encouraged to sow to the Spirit and out of it we reap life everlasting. I believe it is important where we give our finances. Abraham gave tithes to Melchizedek after receiving the bread and wine and God made him rich. Our focus as New Testament priests should be to bring forth the bread and wine. Jesus described the bread as His body which was broken for us and the wine as the New Testament in His blood. When we preach the death, burial and resurrection of Christ we are preaching the New Testament Gospel and have a right to receive tithes of the people.

The second application I want to place my emphasis on is something I felt like the Lord made real to me. You see, the first man Adam sowed to the flesh and for 4000 years we reaped the corruption that was the result of what he sowed. But when you come into the cornfield on the Sabbath day you begin to realize that you are about to reap what Jesus the second man sowed. He took what I had coming so that I could receive what He had coming. According to Isaiah 53, what I had coming was wounding, bruising, chastisement, judgment and corruption. But He bore all of that on the tree.

> *"Surely he hath borne our griefs, and carried our sorrows: yet we did esteem him stricken, smitten of God, and afflicted. But he was wounded for our transgressions, he was bruised for our iniquities: the chastisement of our peace was upon him; and with his stripes we are healed. All we like sheep have gone astray; we have turned every one to his own way; and the LORD hath laid on him the iniquity of us all. He was oppressed, and he was afflicted, yet he opened not his mouth: he is brought as a lamb to the slaughter, and as a sheep before her shearers is dumb, so he openeth not his mouth. He was taken from prison and from judgment: and who shall declare his generation? for he was cut off out of the land of the living: for the transgression of my people was he stricken. And he made his grave with the wicked, and with the rich in his death; because he had done no violence, neither was any deceit in his mouth. Yet it pleased the LORD to bruise him; he hath put him to grief: when thou shalt make his soul an offering for sin, he shall see his seed, he shall prolong his days, and the pleasure of the LORD shall prosper in his hand. He shall see of the travail of his soul, and shall be satisfied: by his knowledge shall my righteous servant justify many; for he shall bear their iniquities."* (Isa. 53: 4-11 KJV)

The first man Adam sowed to the flesh, and out of it we reaped corruption. But the second man, the Lord from heaven sowed to the Spirit and now we reap life everlasting. He took my sickness so I can have His health. He took my death so that I can have His life. He became poor so that I could become rich. He was chastised so that I could have peace. He took my grief so that I could be comforted. According to verse 11, God was so satisfied in the travail of His soul and all He accomplished on the cross, that by the knowledge of what this righteous servant had accomplished in bearing iniquities, He would justify many. He was delivered for our offenses and raised for our justification. Hallelujah, that sure makes this scripture have a positive meaning. Be not deceived! God is not mocked! For what this second man sowed we will surely reap. Come on and walk with Him through this cornfield and feed on what His death accomplished for us. It will truly bring you into a Sabbath rest.

In light of this, the Lord then opened another Scripture to me. Let's take a look at it.

> *"Casting down imaginations, and every high thing that exalteth itself against the knowledge of God, and bringing into captivity every thought to the obedience of Christ;"* (2 Cor. 10:5 KJV)

When the Lord first began to speak to me about this scripture, I thought perhaps He was dealing with me about my thought life. So I began to chase all of my thoughts. I would think "that's not good", and then I would try to bring it back and cast it down. After a short season I was just about worn out with trying keeping tabs on my thoughts. Then the Lord said to me, "I'm not talking about you chasing each individual thought." He said to me, "You have allowed your imagination and thoughts to be captivated by what Adam's disobedience produced rather than focusing on what the obedience of Christ produced." Then He gave me a very powerful key.

> *"For the weapons of our warfare are not carnal, but mighty through God to the pulling down of strong holds;"* (2 Cor. 10:4 KJV)

Our only real fight in the new covenant is the fight of faith. It is the fight to believe what Jesus did was enough. Strongholds are not necessarily demonic powers, but principles that become principalities or parts of our belief system. When I bring my thoughts into captivity to what the obedience of Christ produced it casts down every stronghold and every imagination that lifts itself against what God already knows to be true. Let's look at this verse.

> "Here it is in a nutshell: Just as one person did it wrong and got us in all this trouble with sin and death, another person did it right and got us out of it. But more than just getting us out of trouble, he got us into life! One man said no to God and put many people in the wrong; one man said yes to God and put many in the right. All that passing laws against sin did was produce more lawbreakers. But sin didn't, and doesn't, have a chance in competition with the aggressive forgiveness we call grace. When it's sin versus grace, grace wins hands down. All sin can do is threaten us with death, and that's the end of it. Grace, because God is putting everything together again through the Messiah, invites us into life — a life that goes on and on and on, world without end." (Rom. 5:18-21)

WHEN DEATH BECOMES LIFE

> "So what do we do? Keep on sinning so God can keep on forgiving? I should hope not! If we've left the country where sin is sovereign, how can we still live in our old house there? Or didn't you realize we packed up and left there for good? That is what happened in baptism. When we went under the water, we left the old country of sin behind; when we came up out of the water, we entered into the new country of grace — a new life in a new land!" (Rom. 6:1-3 MSG)

My thoughts had been brought into captivity to the disobedience of Adam, and the result was warfare and turmoil and death, etc. Let's look at some comparisons.

Adam's disobedience in the Garden of Eden caused the ground to be cursed; but obedience of Christ in another garden when He prayed until He sweated great drops of blood redeemed man from the curse of sweat and labor. Now we no longer have to earn God's favor through works.

Because of Adam's disobedience, the Earth brought forth thorns and thistles; but Jesus wore a crown of thorns to redeem us from the torment of pricking thoughts and mental illness.

> Adam's disobedience brought the sentence of death; and the obedience of Christ brought resurrection life.
>
> Adam's disobedience brought sickness; and Jesus' stripes brought healing.
>
> Adam's disobedience brought poverty; but Jesus became poor that I might become rich.
>
> Adam's disobedience brought condemnation; Jesus' obedience brought justification.
>
> Adam's disobedience brought separation; but Jesus' obedience brought reconciliation.
>
> Adam's disobedience brought turmoil; and Jesus' obedience brought rest.
>
> Adam's disobedience got him thrown out of the garden; but the obedience of Christ got us back in the garden. Remember, all of His redemptive work took place in a garden. He was the incorruptible seed that was planted in a new garden to produce a different kind of crop. When Mary saw Him after His resurrection, she said to Him, "Sir, I thought you were the gardener." He in fact was the gardener; and He put

them back in the paradise of God through His redemptive work. Remember what He said to the thief on the cross? "This day you will be with me in paradise." The word paradise is from a Greek word meaning Eden or a garden place.[2]

The wages of Adam's sin was death; but the gift of God, as a result of the obedience of Christ is everlasting life. We could go all night long with lists like this, but you get the idea.

Do you see how we have put all of our thoughts into what Adam's disobedience produced rather than bringing our thoughts into captivity to what the obedience of Christ produced? That is where the real battleground is. It is in our minds. But we will truly be transformed by the renewing of our minds; not by memorizing more scripture or some other religious exercise, but by truly bringing every thought into captivity to what Christ's obedience produced. In this Sabbath Day we reap what He sowed. Praise His dear name!

I think it is important to note at this point that the first Adam was put into a garden that was a beautiful paradise. It was a masterpiece of God's finished work. In Genesis 2 it says, "Thus the heavens and the earth were finished and all the host of them." Right in the middle of a finished work God planted a garden, and he told Adam all he had to do was dress and keep the garden. I could say it like this, God told Adam to dress and keep this finished work. Adam, who was made in the image and likeness of God, failed to believe what God said about him was true. The serpent's temptation was intended to create doubt. God said He made Adam in the image and likeness of Himself; but the serpent said to him and his wife, "In the moment you get enough information about good and evil you can make yourself like God." Adam believed the lie and was damned. That does not mean he went to hell. It means he suffered the consequences of what he believed. The word damned does not necessarily mean to be sentenced to hell. It is the root word for condemnation. Condemnation is still a powerful weapon of the enemy. The same effect that it had on Adam, it has on folks today. Adam's response to this information about good and evil caused him to run from God rather than run to Him. When the voice of the Lord came walking in the garden, Adam hid. God said, "Adam where are you?" Adam said, "I heard your voice and was afraid so I hid myself." Adam became aware of his works instead of God's and it alienated him from fellowship. He said, "I'm naked, I'm ashamed and I need to hide." Isn't that the response of most of the Christian world today? When they hear preaching that comes from the tree of the knowledge of good and evil, or should I say law and legalism, it always invokes the same response: shame, guilt and hiding. But God's response to Adam was, "Who told you that you were naked?" You see, Adam was naked the day before and it didn't bother God. But once he became aware of his nakedness, condemnation set in and he withdrew from God. Isn't that what condemnation does in the hearts of people today? It makes us draw back. Please don't misunderstand me. I am not saying it is alright to sin. I am saying even when you do; don't run from Him, run to Him. That is the purpose of understanding the work of redemption. It is so you can draw near with a true heart in full assurance of faith, having your heart sprinkled from an evil conscience (Heb. 10:22). It is only in this environment that real change transpires. In that ancient garden so long ago, God killed an animal and covered Adam and Eve with coats of skin so the shame of their nakedness would not appear and they would run back to Him instead of running away. For without the shedding of blood there is no remission of sin. That's what the work of the Cross did for us. It clothed us with His righteousness so that now we can come boldly to the throne of grace that we may obtain mercy and find grace to help in time of need. Grace is not greasy. It is our helper. According to the book of Titus, grace is a teacher. It teaches us to deny ungodliness.

> "For the grace of God that bringeth salvation hath appeared to all men, Teaching us that, denying ungodliness and worldly lusts, we should live soberly, righteously, and godly, in this present world;:" (Titus 2:11-12 KJV)

ADAM WHERE ARE YOU?

The first question in the Old Testament was, "Adam where are you?" The first question of the New Testament was, "Where is He who was born King of the Jews?" Please understand that an all-knowing, all-seeing God was not playing hide-and-seek with Adam. God already knew where he was physically located. He was looking for His own image and likeness in a man. He did not see it again until that starry night when in a manger in Bethlehem the King of the Jews had been born. Isn't it amazing that Jesus was wrapped in swaddling clothes and laid in a manger? Why a manger? The answer is, because it was a feed trough. Shepherds, which are symbols of pastors throughout the Bible, were watching their flocks by night. There are many pastors today that are still in a season of darkness and do not know what to feed their flocks. So they feed them on politics, self-help programs, entertainment, news and world events, or legalistic, old covenant preaching. It has not and will not produce life in the sheep. Only bringing them to the feed trough of Bethlehem's manger and feeding them a steady diet of Lamb and what the death of this Lamb produced will bring them peace on earth and goodwill to men. That must be the message of true shepherds in this hour. We must fill the trough with corn from this Sabbath cornfield. We must declare that a corn of wheat fell into the earth and died to bring forth much fruit, and that what He did was enough.

Remember, Adam's problem began with an eating disorder. He ate from the wrong tree. Much of what is shared over pulpits today has the same recipe for failure. We feed them the sugar-coated Twinkies or the greasy potato chips of spiritual junk food that draws the crowds and fills the stomach temporarily. It gives them the temporary euphoria of a sugar high and they bounce off the walls for an hour-and-a-half only to have the crash of disappointment, because there's no substance in what they're eating. At the same time, their spiritual arteries are being clogged with the fat and debris that causes hearts to be hardened and spiritual heart failure. We must change our diet. If we ate our way into this problem, we can certainly eat our way out.

CORN IN EGYPT

Remember, in Genesis 42 the children of Israel were enslaved to the bondage of Egypt for hundreds of years because of a famine in their land. But God sent Joseph to preserve their lives. Joseph is a type of our heavenly Joseph, Jesus Christ, and was sold by his brothers into slavery much like Jesus in the New Testament was rejected by His own. The sufferings of Joseph have a tremendous parallel to the sufferings of Jesus. Because of his father's favor Joseph was given a coat of many colors that made his brothers jealous, resulting in them selling him into slavery. Likewise, Jesus in the New Testament was given the favor of His father that made the scribes and Pharisees jealous, resulting in Him being handed over to Pilot. The coat of Joseph symbolizes with its rainbow colors the new covenant. Remember when God made a covenant with Noah? He gave him a symbol of a rainbow. Our heavenly Joseph, Jesus Christ, is clothed with the favor of His father in His new covenant coat of many colors. Just like Joseph was sold into prison and falsely accused, so too Jesus was falsely accused and sold. Joseph was stripped of his coat, and Jesus was stripped of His garments. Joseph was thrown into the pit, and Jesus went down into the pit. While men meant this for evil, God meant it for good. Was that not the conclusion of Joseph when he finally revealed himself to his brethren? He said to them, "You meant it for evil, but God meant it for good. He has sent me ahead of you to preserve your life." God in His infinite wisdom and provision has now exalted to the throne a greater Joseph. He is now ruler of all the land and there is corn in abundance. When the famine gets bad enough it will drive people to seek out the One who now has a plentiful supply of corn. When Jacob learned there was corn in Egypt, he decided to send his sons to see if it was true. Can you imagine the heart of Joseph as he sees his brothers for the first time in many years? He has not seen them since they sold him into slavery. Yet his heart is overwhelmed because the need for corn is what will reconcile them. He discovers that his father and his full brother Benjamin are yet alive. His desire is to bring all of them to the place of his provision. He devises a plan that will accomplish his purpose. He sends them back for his father and brother with their sacks full of corn and their money returned to them in their sacks. He also told his servants to put his silver cup in the mouth of their sack.

This is a powerful picture of the work of Jesus' redemption. The corn speaks of Jesus' death and suffering while the returning of their money speaks of the truth that you cannot buy redemption. The empty cup in the mouth of the sack speaks of the truth that Christ has already drunk the cup of suffering for us. Many today preach the sufferings of Christ as if they are a pattern that we must follow. Jesus was a pattern son in his earth walk. But Jesus was not the pattern Son in His redemptive work. He did not suffer to show us how to suffer. He suffered to redeem us from suffering. He paid the debt He did not owe; I owed a debt I could not pay. Only His suffering could be redemptive, because He had no wages of sin coming. He suffered and died to redeem us from sin, sickness, poverty and death. Everything that He secured for us in His redemptive work, I do not have to pay for again. Remember the example of Judas. He had the price of redemption in his hand, the thirty pieces of silver, because he did not remember the words of Jesus the night before when he took the bread and wine and gave it to his betrayers (I Cor. 11:23). Remember just about all of them would betray Him before the week was over. Jesus said this is my body that was broken for you. Judas did not discern the Lord's body, in other words he did not understand that the death of Jesus was his death. He went out and hanged himself on a tree. However, his death was not redemptive nor was his suffering required. If Judas would have waited a couple of hours, the hanging of Jesus would have been his hanging. Let us not be guilty of thinking that what Jesus did was not enough. Let us not throw away the price of redemption that is within our grasp and try to do all over again what Jesus completely paid in full. Only the death of the spotless Lamb will be accepted. The suffering we have not been redeemed from is when men speak evil against us or persecute us for righteousness sake. Imagine the surprise in the eyes of Joseph's brothers when they realized their money was in the sack and the king's empty cup was also there. It will be much like the surprise in the hearts of God's people today when they realize that He has already drunk a cup of suffering for us, and that we cannot purchase our own redemption. Silver in the scripture speaks of redemption. Joseph returned his brothers' money signifying that only he and he alone could purchase and redeem them from suffering and from famine. This event was the beginning of the reconciliation and reunion between him and his family. He later, during the feast he prepared for them, revealed himself to them. Jesus likewise is revealing Himself to us as we continue to feast at His table.

You can eat your way out of the problem. One more example of this is when the children of Israel got ready to leave Egyptian bondage. God told them to take a lamb out from among the sheep and the goats and to apply the blood to the doorposts of their houses. He also told them to take the lamb inside the house and eat it in the night roasted with fire. What they were about to eat would give them the strength to leave Egyptian bondage. Many have erroneously taught that the blood on the doorpost told the death Angel this house escapes. But that is not what the blood said to the death Angel. The blood that was on the doorpost said to the death Angel there has already been a death exacted here. The death of the lamb was the death of the firstborn. That is why the feast is called Passover. In the new covenant Jesus did not die so I would not have to. He died because I did have to. He was God's method of getting rid of who I was in Adam. He did not just die for me, He died as me! I was crucified with Christ. If I will feed on this Lamb and His death, it will empower me to leave all of the bondage of Egypt behind me. The children of Israel fed on the lamb. They also ate the manna in the wilderness, and they drank water from the smitten rock. All of these are pictures of Christ. He was the Lamb and the true Bread. He was the Rock that followed them in the wilderness, and there was not a feeble one among them. Not one among them was sick. If this could happen in the Old Testament as a type and shadow, how much more in the New Testament, if we get on the right diet, should it not remove sickness and feebleness from among us? Is this not what happens at the communion table when we discern that His death made me worthy to eat the bread and drink the wine that removes the weakness and sickness from my body? Jesus said, "Except you eat my flesh and drink my blood you have no life in you." The Bible is full of stories like this one that show us that we can eat our way out of the problem. Thank God there was corn to eat on the Sabbath day.

THE GARDEN AND THE WILDERNESS

Isn't it amazing that Adam had a garden and because he failed to guard and keep this garden, it became a wilderness? The garden could also be called a finished work because in Genesis 2 it says, "Thus the heavens and the earth were finished, and all the host of them." God planted a garden in the midst of a finished work, but because Adam did not guard and keep the finished work, it became a waste-howling wilderness. But the second Adam shows up in a wilderness after He is baptized by John the Baptist and undergoes the same temptations as the first Adam. The serpent said to Him, "If you be the Son of God, command these stones to be turned into bread." Now isn't it amazing that the temptation of the second Adam has to do with eating and identity? Remember, the first Adam ate from the tree of the knowledge of good and evil which symbolized the law and it made Adam question his identity. He no longer believed he was in the image and likeness of God. The second Adam is being tempted with the exact same temptations except using a different symbol. The first words of Satan to Jesus, "If you be the son of God," was a question of identity. The second thing Satan says to Jesus is, "Command these stones to be turned into bread." In places throughout the word of God stones represent the law.

> "But if the ministration of death, written and engraven in stones, was glorious, so that the children of Israel could not sted-fastly behold the face of Moses for the glory of his countenance; which glory was to be done away:" (2 Cor. 3:7 KJV)

In this text the law is called the "ministration of death". The temptation of Jesus was to command the stone of the law to be turned into bread. The devil was trying to do to the second Adam what he had done to the first one. He was trying to get Jesus to feed on the knowledge of good and evil and to find

His identity based on His performance. He was trying to get Jesus to make the dead letter of the law a part of His daily diet.

> *"And the commandment, which was ordained to life, I found to be unto death."* (Rom. 7:10 KJV)

> *"Is the law then against the promises of God? God forbid: for if there had been a law given which could have given life, verily righteousness should have been by the law."* (Gal. 3:21 KJV)

You see, the stone of the law could not give life. Jesus had found the only true source of life that really existed was living by every word that would proceed out of the mouth of God. Jesus was living out of a relationship instead of rules. It was a true father-son relationship called the unforced rhythm of grace. Jesus had found a living and vibrant relationship with His father that became the very staple of life, as important as our daily bread. Our prayer should be, "Give us this day our daily bread. Teach us Lord to live out of our relationship with You, to feed on the true Bread that came down from heaven. The fresh manna that is new every morning and not the stale bread of religious performance." We have become victims of identity theft by trying to turn the cold stones of the law into bread. Jesus resisted this temptation by believing the word that had just proceeded out of the mouth of His father. What was the preceding word? "This is my son in whom I am well pleased." The father had just uttered these words in front of the multitudes as soon as Jesus emerged from the waters of baptism. The approval of a father will always empower a son. Sons get their identities from their fathers. The Father said, "You are my Son in whom I am well pleased." The devil said, "If you be the Son." The devil was challenging the preceding word. He was challenging the word that God had just spoken much like he had challenged the word that God had spoken concerning the first Adam. The difference this time was that the last Adam did not believe the lie. This time Jesus knew exactly who He was. He was not going to eat from the cold stones of the law to get His identity. He would instead turn to the warm words of His father and overcome every temptation that would follow.

All sin flows from a mistaken identity. Adam believed the lie and sin was the result. We know the truth and the truth makes us free. Right believing will produce right living. Because we are in Christ we have the Father's approval. The Apostle Paul wrote Timothy and told him to study to show himself approved unto God, a workman that needeth not to be ashamed, rightly dividing the word of truth. I think when we study the word what we must do is study to see that, because of the work of Calvary, we have been accepted in the Beloved and we have been approved by God. We have been given the gift of righteousness and we have the Father's approval. Rightly dividing the word of truth does not suggest to me that we must learn the difference between Greek and Hebrew. It means we know how to discern what is truth in relationship to the old covenant and what is truth in the new covenant. The old covenant tells you what is wrong with you, and the new covenant tells you what is right. The old covenant disqualifies us, and the new covenant qualifies. In the old covenant the letter kills. In the new covenant the Spirit gives life. We must learn to live by every word that proceeds from the mouth of God. Understanding what the corn on the Sabbath symbolizes puts us in a posture to receive God's favor. Understanding that He was crushed, sifted, bruised as the true corn of wheat that fell into the earth and died, shows me what qualified me to receive the Father's approval. Remember, He was feeding His disciples on the Sabbath day in the cornfield something more than just natural grain. For those with a spiritual eye to see, He was feeding them on what His death would produce for them. He was giving them the true staple and bread of life. He was feeding them on what His death would produce for them. It would put them back in the favor of God with the Father's approval. It would ultimately take a waste-howling wilderness, the result of Adam not keeping and guarding the garden, and begin the process of turning it back into a garden. God's plan is a plan of restoration. The wilderness that the second Adam showed up in was an un-kept garden. If you are going to restore the garden, you cannot plant the same seed and hope to get a different crop. In that wilderness temptation the second Adam did not fail. He began the process of reversing the curse so that we can live in the unlimited garden of provision that His death exacted for us. He was the incorruptible seed of God that would be planted in a new garden, and from this incorruptible seed produce a whole crop of incorruptible sons of God.

Isn't it amazing that even the feasts of Israel are always surrounding a harvest? At Passover they offered a wave of sheath of first fruits symbolizing that the seed that was planted was now resurrected and it was the first fruits, a guarantee that a harvest would follow. The Feast of Pentecost represented the first fruits of the wheat harvest. The Feast of Tabernacles also known as the Feast of Ingathering was celebrated in the fall and was the harvest season of the corn, the wine and the oil. I believe we are about to celebrate one of the greatest Feasts of Ingathering and a harvest unparalleled in human history. The result of that incorruptible seed that was planted in the earth over two millenniums ago will be an unprecedented coming harvest. If we as leaders can bring our disciples into this cornfield and allow them to feed from a Sabbath rest we will see a crop like no other generation has ever seen. It is not an accident that everything Jesus does in His redemptive work He does it in a garden. He prays in the garden of Gethsemane until He sweats, He sweats until he bleeds. If one drop of blood from the divine brow ever touches a cursed earth, it will put the curse that says you must earn your bread by the sweat of your brow in reverse. No more works trying to earn God's favor. He was crucified in a garden. His tomb is in a garden. After all, where else would you plant this incorruptible seed except in a garden? When Mary saw Jesus after His resurrection she said to Him, "Sir, I thought you were the gardener." He in fact was the gardener, and the first fruits of those that slept. He put us back in a finished work where all we have to do is guard and keep what He has accomplished in His death, burial and resurrection. We are now the harvest coming forth in the power of His resurrection.

*"We are only God's coworkers. **You are God's garden**, not ours; you are God's building, not ours."* (1 Cor. 3:9 TLB)

Have Ye Not Heard What David Did When He Was Hungry?

"But when the Pharisees saw it, they said unto him, Behold, thy disciples do that which is not lawful to do upon the sabbath day. But he said unto them, Have ye not read what David did, when he was an hungred, and they that were with him; How he entered into the house of God, and did eat the shewbread, which was not lawful for him to eat, neither for them which were with him, but only for the priests?" (Matt. 12:2-4 KJV)

"Then came David to Nob to Ahimelech the priest: and Ahimelech was afraid at the meeting of David, and said unto him, Why art thou alone, and no man with thee? And David said unto Ahimelech the priest, The king hath commanded me a business, and hath said unto me, Let no man know any thing of the business whereabout I send thee, and what I have commanded thee: and I have appointed my servants to such and such a place. Now therefore what is under thine hand? give me five loaves of bread in mine hand, or what there is present. And the priest answered David, and said, There is no common bread under mine hand, but there is hallowed bread; if the young men have kept themselves at least from women. And David answered the priest, and said unto him, Of a truth women have been kept from us about these three days, since I came out, and the vessels of the young men are holy, and the bread is in a manner common, yea, though it were sanctified this day in the vessel. So the priest gave him hallowed bread: for there was no bread there but the shewbread, that was taken from before the Lord, to put hot bread in the day when it was taken away. Now a certain man of the servants of Saul was there that day, detained before the Lord; and his name was Doeg, an Edomite, the chiefest of the herdmen that belonged to

Saul. And David said unto Ahimelech, And is there not here under thine hand spear or sword? for I have neither brought my sword nor my weapons with me, because the king's business required haste. And the priest said, The sword of Goliath the Philistine, whom thou slewest in the valley of Elah, behold, it is here wrapped in a cloth behind the ephod: if thou wilt take that, take it: for there is no other save that here. And David said, There is none like that; give it me." (I Sam. 21:1-10 KJV)

The story of David is also a story of the greater Son of David, our heavenly King Jesus. Let us make some comparisons. In the above story, King David was fleeing for his life from Saul. He had been anointed king by the Prophet Samuel and was simply waiting for the old regime under the reign of Saul to pass off the scene. He was the king not yet recognized. Does that sound familiar? The Pharisees of Jesus' day were pursuing Him much like Saul pursued David to take his life. They perceived Jesus as a threat to their reign. Jesus, much like David, was king yet unrecognized. He was not only just a king unrecognized, Jesus as well as David was a King Priest. Because they were priests they had a legal right to eat from the table of showbread. The Pharisees are quoting the law to Jesus, while He is trying to show them the heart of grace. The Pharisees believe that their religion and inflexible rituals are at stake here. In the following verse, Jesus tells them He prefers a flexible heart to an inflexible ritual. Jesus is the new King Priest after the order of Melchizedek and this new King Priest does not operate from carnal commandments. He operates by the power of an endless life. He is introducing the unforced rhythms of grace. He was actually fulfilling the duties of the priest by giving his disciples fresh bread on the Sabbath.

"Jesus said, 'Really? Didn't you ever read what David and his companions did when they were hungry, how they entered the sanctuary and ate fresh bread off the altar, bread that no one but priests were allowed to eat? And didn't you ever read in God's Law that priests carrying out their Temple duties break

Sabbath rules all the time and it's not held against them?
There is far more at stake here than religion. If you had any
idea what this Scripture meant — 'I prefer a flexible heart to
an inflexible ritual' — you wouldn't be nitpicking like this. The
Son of Man is no lackey to the Sabbath; he's in charge.'" (Matt.
12:3-8 MSG)

Remember, David and his companions were fleeing from Saul. They became hungry and entered the sanctuary. David asked the priests if they had any bread to which they replied, "There is no bread here except the showbread which is hallowed." The table of Showbread had two stacks of six loaves of bread. The word Showbread in Smith's Bible Dictionary is defined as "the bread of face," or "the bread through which God is seen." When we take a closer look at the bread, we understand that it is once again a revelation of the death burial and resurrection of Jesus Christ. Jesus is the true Bread. The first stack of six loaves speaks of the work of Jesus. The second stack speaks of my identification with His work.

First stack of bread:	Second stack of bread:
He was	I was
1. Crucified	1. Crucified with Him
2. Died	2. Died with Him
3. Buried	3. Buried with Him
4. Quickened	4. Quickened with Him
5. Raised	5. Raised with Him
6. Seated	6. Seated with Him

You see, He did not just die for me. He died as me. He did not die so I would not have to; he died because I had to. His death was my death. His crucifixion was my crucifixion. I was buried with Him in baptism. I was quickened and made alive with His life. I have His resurrection life living in me. I am right now seated with Him in the heavenly places according to Ephesians 2. Six things we are made partakers of in the redemptive work of Christ.

Perhaps David penned these words when he was fleeing from Saul.

You serve me a six-course dinner right in front of my enemies.
You revive my drooping head; my cup brims with blessing. (Ps. 23:5 MSG)

Once again we are pointed to something to feed on. Just like the corn was a type of feeding on the death, burial and resurrection of Jesus Christ, so also is the table of Showbread. Everything about the activities Jesus did on the Sabbath point to what will bring a real rest in the life of the believer. A new King Priest has arisen, and He has a legal right to feed His disciples a steady diet of the finished work of the cross. And it does not profane the Sabbath. It is interesting to note that there is a total of 12 loaves of bread and there are 12 disciples. Twelve is the number of divine government in the scripture. Jesus was establishing a new form of governing. He would do it on the foundation of the apostles and prophets, Jesus Christ himself being the Chief Cornerstone. This new kingdom would not be established on the inflexible rules of the law or a religious ritual. It would be established upon a flexible heart of love. These disciples would become apostles who would become part of a kingdom much greater than David's. They would be much like David's rag tag team of misfits and rejects that would later become his mighty men. From these 12 men who went forth preaching the gospel of the kingdom, was birthed the beginnings of the kingdom of God and the present reign of Jesus Christ. They went from house to house breaking bread. That was so much more than just sitting at a table eating a physical meal. It was breaking the bread of His death, burial and resurrection. That was their constant message. As often as they came together they ate the bread and drank the wine of the new covenant. Jesus said to His disciples, "I will not drink wine again until I drink it new with you in my Father's kingdom." In Acts 2, in an upper room, probably the same upper room Jesus had given them communion in just 50 days prior, the new wine of the Holy Spirit was poured out. Jesus had kept His word and was now drinking new wine in the kingdom with His disciples. They were celebrating the coming of the kingdom. The Kingdom of God is not meat and drink. It is righteousness, peace and joy, and it's located in the Holy Ghost. If you are filled with the Holy Ghost, then you are filled with the Kingdom of God. You are filled with kingdom purpose and potential. "Go ye therefore and make disciples of all nations" is now the mandate of every spirit filled Christian on the planet.

THE SWORD OF GOLIATH

One final thought as we close this chapter. When David came to the priest at Nob, he asked the priest, "Do you have here any weapons?" The priest replied, "The only weapon we have here is the sword of Goliath hidden behind the ephod." Now imagine what this sword meant to David. He had brought it there many years ago right after the victory over Goliath. It reminded him of a past victory. It reminded him of the day the children of Israel sang, "Saul has killed his thousands but David has killed his ten thousands." It was the day he was perceived as a conquering king. What a comfort that sword must have been in the hand of David as he wrapped his hand around it. It reminded him of the promise of God that one day he would be king. He was now fleeing from the present regime that was trying to kill him. He would be reduced to dwelling in a cave that was much like a tomb. Out of this dark cave of death would emerge a great king. Isn't that a powerful picture of our Lord Jesus Christ, the greater son of David?

The Philistines began to chant, "Give us one man to fight our champion and if he wins we will serve you. If our champion wins you will serve us." Remember, Goliath was his name. He had six fingers and six toes. Six is the number of fallen man; so Goliath represents fallen man under the control of the devil. Our heavenly David through the work of the cross has defeated every enemy. He defeated the devil and crucified who I was in Adam. Jesus was crucified at Golgotha, the place of the skull. Some say that Golgotha is derived from the name Goliath of Gath. Legend has it that the head of Goliath was buried at the place where the cross would be erected.

Our heavenly David has defeated every enemy through His death, burial and resurrection. When we are fleeing for our lives and it looks like the promise of God has failed, we must go to our High Priest and ask Him for the bread that is hallowed. When we are discouraged we must ask for the sword of Goliath. It is a trophy of faith, a reminder of a past victory that will sustain you. David did not get that sword to kill Saul. He had opportunities to kill King Saul, but refused to touch God's anointed. That sword was a reminder to David of a past victory. As he lay in that wet, damp cave he must have reached over and patted that sword and said, "I don't have to fight in this battle, the battle has already been won." It was only a matter of time until David would come out of that cave of death to be exalted to the throne. Our heavenly David has come forth out of the cave of death and is presently reigning. When you are faced with the disappointments of life and it does not seem like you are reigning in life, go to the house of God and feed on the true Bread, the finished work. Reach for the sword of Goliath, not so you can fight in this battle, but so you can be reminded that the battle has already been won. Wrap your hand around this great trophy. It is only a matter of time until you come forth and reign in life. Take a walk with Him through this cornfield, and it will bring you into a perpetual Sabbath rest.

ENDNOTES

1. J.B. Jackson, *Dictionary of Scripture Proper Names,* 3rd edition (Loizeaux Brothers, Neptune, NJ. 1957) Pg. 9.

2. James Strong, *Strong's Exhaustive Concordance of the Bible,* (Dugan Publishers, Inc. Gordonsville,TN. 1890) Pg. 54.

Chapter Three

THE WITHERED HAND

*"And, behold, there was a man which had his hand withered.
And they asked him, saying, is it lawful to heal on the Sabbath
days? That they might accuse him. And he said unto them,
What man shall there be among you, that shall have one sheep,
and if it fall into a pit on the sabbath day, will he not lay hold
on it, and lift it out? How much then is a man better than a
sheep? Wherefore it is lawful to do well on the sabbath days.
Then saith he to the man, Stretch forth thine hand. And he
stretched it forth; and it was restored whole, like as the other."*
(Matt. 12:10-13 KJV)

I t is my hope that by this stage of the book you can clearly see that I am not
taking anything away from the fact that Jesus really healed these people
2000 years ago. But truth is like an onion, the more you peel it the more
layers you find. My attempt is simply to unravel what these incredible miracles
of the Sabbath prophetically speak. The Scriptures declare that if the things
which Jesus had done were written in a book, I reckon that the world could
not contain the books. It is therefore my conclusion that the few miracles that
are listed throughout the Scriptures probably had a greater meaning than just
surface truth. They were chosen by the Holy Spirit to convey to us perhaps a
deeper meaning. Let us then unravel this miracle.

It is widely held among many that the hand is a symbol of the five-fold ministry; primarily because there are five ministry gifts listed in the book of Ephesians.

> *"And he gave some, apostles; and some, prophets; and some, evangelists; and some, pastors and teachers; For the perfecting of the saints, for the work of the ministry, for the edifying of the body of Christ: Till we all come in the unity of the faith, and of the knowledge of the Son of God, unto a perfect man, unto the measure of the stature of the fulness of Christ: That we henceforth be no more children, tossed to and fro, and carried about with every wind of doctrine, by the sleight of men, and cunning craftiness, whereby they lie in wait to deceive; But speaking the truth in love, may grow up into him in all things, which is the head, even Christ:"* (Eph. 4:11-15 KJV)

Scripture also connects the ministry to His hand in chapter one of the book of Revelation when He declares the messengers to the church are in His right hand. The body of Christ has many members, all of them with different functions. Let's look at the function of the hand. Let us not say to the hand I have no need of you.

While most churches embrace the office of the pastor, teacher and evangelist, some do not. They go as far as to say that apostles and prophets ended in the days of Jesus. The Scriptures themselves declare how long these five ascension gifts would be in operation. Verse 13 of the same chapter declares that these ministries will operate till we all come to the unity of the faith and the knowledge of the Son of God unto a perfect man, unto the measure of the stature of the fullness of Christ. I don't think we have arrived at this point in our experience as of yet. It is because of this kind of thinking that we have failed to equip the saints for the work of service.

> *"...for the equipping of the saints for the work of service, to the building up of the body of Christ;"* (Eph. 4:12-13 NASU)

Perhaps this withered hand pictures a powerless ministry and powerless saints that no longer has the ability to help sheep get out of the pit.

Many great books have already been written defining the role of each one of these ministries, so I will try to be brief with my description. For example, let's take that the thumb may represent the apostle because he is the balance of the whole hand. Can you imagine trying to grasp a utensil to eat with or a cup to drink from without your thumb? Is it any wonder that a great deal of the church world is starved spiritually and are so readily willing to cut off the thumb of the body of Christ that could help them grasp the spiritual food that could bring them to maturity? As we see in the early church the primary function of the apostle was to govern the church. It is a sad indictment in this hour but so many churches are governed by a democracy rather than a theocracy. It is much like a family being governed by its children rather than the parents. If the children were in control they would demand French fries and ice cream for every meal. While that may satisfy their hunger temporarily, it ultimately produces in them a deficiency, weakness and sickness. It is a tragedy when congregations dictate to men of God what they can or cannot preach from the pulpits. And while I do believe that God uses elders and deacons in local church settings as well as a Presbytery of ministry to help govern the people of God, it was never in the heart of God for the laity to govern. Can you imagine a board voting the apostle Paul out of his position? You see, God sets these gifts in the body as it pleases Him, not as it pleases us. I would not want to find myself in opposition to the person that God chose to watch for my soul. Some churches change pastors as often as they change light bulbs. Men of God are in fear for their jobs and cannot truly preach what they think God is saying for fear of being fired. But I believe God is healing this withered hand and real apostles are coming on the scene again. One of their functions is to govern.

The pointing finger to me represents the prophet because one of his functions is to guide. He is the one who points the finger and says this is the way, walk in it.

The middle finger represents the evangelist because he has the longest outreach and his function is to gather.

The ring finger represents the pastor because he is the one in which we should be in covenant. His function is to guard.

The little finger represents the teacher. He is the smallest of the fingers and has the ability to get in your ear and scratch it when it itches. His function is to ground us in the Word.

In summary:

- the apostle governs
- the prophet guides
- the evangelist gathers
- the pastor guards
- the teacher grounds

In the text above, this hand is withered. It has no power and is ineffective. They asked Jesus if it was lawful to heal on the Sabbath day, not because they wanted to help the people, but because they wanted to accuse Jesus. Jesus responded by saying, "What man among you shall there be that shall have one sheep, and if it fall into a pit on the Sabbath day, will he not lay hold on it, and lift it out?" (Matt.12:11) Now immediately I began to think that Jesus is talking not only about a barnyard creature called a sheep but something much bigger of a spiritual significance. Perhaps He's talking about the people we are shepherds over, our flocks. They are His people and the sheep of His pasture. He confirms this thought in Matt. 12:12 when He says "How much then is a man better than a sheep." Perhaps these people are in a pit because ministry is not flowing from the posture of rest or from the perspective of the Sabbath. Their ministry is not flowing from the finished work of the cross. Therefore, it is powerless and withered. The apostle Paul said the preaching of the cross is to them who are perishing foolishness, but to us who believe it is the power of God unto salvation. As ministry begins to return to preaching the cross instead of all kinds of side issues, I believe there will be a manifestation of God's power restored to the church. God is bringing forth a new breed of ministry in this hour that is not afraid to preach the gospel. Much of what has flooded our pulpits has been issues of politics, self-help programs, psychological manipulation and just empty rhetoric with no biblical basis. Is it any wonder the sheep have fallen into a pit? Let's explore some things the Scriptures have to say about a pit.

> *"For a whore is a deep ditch; and a strange woman is a narrow pit."* (Prov. 23:27 KJV)

Perhaps this Scripture is not talking about some harlot on a street corner, but instead it is talking about a harlot religious system that is a meat market parade of flesh. It is more of an entertainment-based man-centered religious system that is in a competition to see who can build the best little brothel in town. They will moan and groan for an hour on Sunday morning, as long as the money is on the table when you leave. Somehow we leave there feeling used, disappointed and abused, never really having the longing of our soul satisfied. We come longing for intimacy with Jesus and leave never really having an encounter with Him. We are pointed to religion instead of a relationship to the law rather than love. We experienced a momentary excitement, but not real fulfillment that comes from being in a marriage relationship with our King. We have learned how to practice safe church and we are in a pit as a result of it. Let us explore the message of the harlot in the book of Revelation.

> *"How much she hath glorified herself, and lived deliciously, so much torment and sorrow give her: for she saith in her heart, I sit a queen, and am no widow, and shall see no sorrow."* (Rev. 18:7 KJV)

Her message is, I am a queen and I am not a widow. She refuses to acknowledge that her first husband Adam is dead. Because she does not understand that her first husband Adam is dead she gives a cup full of suffering to her followers. She does not understand that Jesus drank the cup of suffering for every man when He was on the cross. It was there that He redeemed us from the curse of the law and from the suffering that accompanied that covenant. He delivered us from every curse, including generational curses.

> *"In those days they shall say no more, The fathers have eaten a sour grape, and the children's teeth are set on edge. But every one shall die for his own iniquity: every man that eateth the sour grape, his teeth shall be set on edge. Behold, the days come, saith the Lord, that I will make a new covenant with the house of Israel, and with the house of Judah:"* (Jer. 31:29-31 KJV)

In this text the reason the children's teeth are set on edge is because they expected the sins of the fathers to be visited to the third and fourth generation. But the prophet clearly puts this in the context of the new covenant in verse 31. Under the old covenant the sins of the fathers were visited to the third and fourth generation. In the new covenant God said your sins and iniquities I will remember no more. Why did He say that? Because one man Jesus died for all of our iniquities. He was wounded for our transgression and bruised for our iniquities. The chastisement of our peace was on Him (Isaiah 53). When He was on the cross He cried out, "I thirst" and they brought him vinegar to drink. Vinegar comes from sour grapes. What He was doing was taking every curse and every generational curse that was put on us by becoming the one man that would die to redeem us from the curse of the law so that no longer would our teeth be set on edge with an expectancy of judgment. His next words were, "It is finished". Every demand that the law could put on us of suffering and impending judgment had been finished, and the righteous demand of God was fully satisfied. When God viewed the cross He said I have seen the travail of His soul and I am satisfied. Folks, we have been redeemed from sin, sickness, poverty and death. God is not using any of those to process us into His image. Do not drink the bitter cup of suffering that this harlot system tries to offer you because Jesus already drank the cup for us. Remember in the previous chapter that the king's empty cup was in the mouth of Benjamin's sack of corn. It symbolized the fact that you have been redeemed from the suffering that is associated with the curse of the law. The function of valid five-fold new covenant ministry is to develop and mature the new creation man. We are not trying to kill the old man, nor are we trying to get Adam to behave. We have reckoned him to be dead. The old covenant was written to the old man to try to get him to behave. The new covenant is written to the new man. If you are preaching to Adam, you are preaching to the wrong man. It is much like the mistake of Abraham who thought he could fluff and buff Ishmael to make him look like Abraham in the face, but inside he had the heart of an Egyptian beating in his breast. You see, the old covenant could change a man's behavior, but the new covenant would change a man's heart. It is the difference between being conformed and being transformed. Paul said in Romans 12, "Be not conformed to this world but be transformed by the renewing of your mind." When Paul used the terminology "be not conformed to this world", he was not talking about what we call worldly. When I was growing up in classical Pentecost the term worldly meant you had gone back to wearing clothes that were in fashion or going to the movies or some other form of what we called sin. But the context was not dealing with what we call sin. It was dealing with the idea of a passing age. The word world in this text is from a Greek word meaning an age. The age that was passing was the old covenant mosaic economy. It was the message of conformity because it dealt with external behavior modification; while the new covenant of grace would deal with the internal heart of a man. Please note this verse from this translation.

> "And stop assuming an outward expression that does not come
> from within you and is not representative of what you are in
> your inner being but is patterned after this age; but change
> your outward expression to one that comes from within and
> is representative of your inner being, by the renewing of your
> mind, resulting in your putting to the test what is the will of
> God, the good and well-pleasing and complete will, and having
> found that it meets specifications, place your approval upon it."
> (Rom. 12:2 WUEST)

You see both new covenant and old covenant preachers desire to see change. What is in question is how that is accomplished. The old covenant way is conformity to rules while the new covenant way is transformation through relationship.

Is There Anything New

Let's look at the desperate cry of Solomon in the book of Ecclesiastes for a change. Please note that when Solomon writes the book of Ecclesiastes he is looking for life under the sun. He is looking for life under the heavens. He is a lost soul looking for what is the essence of life and what is the purpose for the sons of men under the heavens. He concludes that it is all vanity and vexation of spirit and there is no life under the sun. When he writes the Song of Solomon he is no longer looking for life under the sun, but he has found life in the Son. He is not looking for life under the heavens. He has found life in the heavens.

> *"The words of the Preacher, the son of David, king in Jerusa-*
> *lem. Vanity of vanities, saith the Preacher, vanity of vanities;*
> *all is vanity. What profit hath a man of all his labour which*
> *he taketh under the sun? One generation passeth away, and*
> *another generation cometh: but the earth abideth for ever.*
> *The sun also ariseth, and the sun goeth down, and hasteth to*
> *his place where he arose. The wind goeth toward the south,*
> *and turneth about unto the north; it whirleth about continu-*
> *ally, and the wind returneth again according to his circuits.*
> *All the rivers run into the sea; yet the sea is not full; unto the*
> *place from whence the rivers come, thither they return again.*
> *All things are full of labour; man cannot utter it: the eye is*
> *not satisfied with seeing, nor the ear filled with hearing. The*
> *thing that hath been, it is that which shall be; and that which*
> *is done is that which shall be done: and there is no new thing*
> *under the sun. Is there anything whereof it may be said, See,*

this is new? it hath been already of old time, which was before us." (Eccl. 1:1-10 KJV)

"That which is crooked cannot be made straight: and that which is wanting cannot be numbered." (Eccl. 1:15 KJV)

The desperate question of this king who was living under an old covenant was, is there anything anywhere that you can say see, this is new? The utter discouragement in his voice as he declared that which is crooked cannot be made straight, demands from us a new covenant answer. In the new covenant we are not living life under the sun but we are living a life in the SON. We are not living a life under the heavens we are living life in the heavens. It is in that place that we can answer the question of Solomon with an entire list of new things as well as the indwelling transforming power of the Holy Spirit that can in fact take that which is crooked and make it straight. Let us look at a few of these.

"Therefore if any man be in Christ, he is a new creature: old things are passed away; behold, all things are become new." (2 Cor. 5:17 KJV)

A life in Christ is a life in the Son. By virtue of our new birth we were placed in Christ where we became partakers of the divine nature. He did not give us a law that we could keep. He gave us a life that could keep us. In the new covenant Jesus gave His life for us, and then He gave His life to us. Now it is our privilege to let Him live His life through us. It is not human effort or self-help. It is something brand new; a new life in a new land.

*"Here it is in a nutshell: Just as one person did it wrong and got us in all this trouble with sin and death, another person did it right and got us out of it. But more than just getting us out of trouble, **he got us into life!** One man said no to God and put many people in the wrong; one man said yes to God*

*and put many in the right. All that passing laws against sin did was produce more lawbreakers. But sin didn't, and doesn't, have a chance in competition with the aggressive forgiveness we call grace. When it's sin versus grace, grace wins hands down. All sin can do is threaten us with death, and that's the end of it. Grace, because God is putting everything together again through the Messiah, **invites us into life — a life that goes on and on and on, world without end.***

When Death Becomes Life

*So what do we do? Keep on sinning so God can keep on forgiving? I should hope not! If we've left the country where sin is sovereign, how can we still live in our old house there? Or didn't you realize we packed up and left there for good? That is what happened in baptism. When we went under the water, we left the old country of sin behind; when we came up out of the water, **we entered into the new country of grace — a new life in a new land!***" (Rom. 5:18-6:3 MSG)

How is that for an answer, Solomon? That which is crooked can be made straight! The cycles of repetitive, destructive, sinful behavior can be broken. Please note that everything in this first chapter of Ecclesiastes is dealing with repetitive cycles. The sun arises and it goes down. The wind moves about in cycles. The rivers run into the sea, yet the sea is not full. They return to their place by evaporation and repetitive cycles. In utter frustration he declares the thing which has been, is what is going to be. He seems to be locked into repetitive behavior. If you have ever noticed, many times it seems like the same problems follow families like eating disorders, substance abuse, sexual dysfunction, poverty and a whole list of other problems of repetitive behavior. They are learned behaviors that I call principalities. A principality is not always a demonic spirit. It is a principle that becomes part of our belief system that governs our lives. But these cycles can be broken. One person can change the course of history for the entire family simply by making a decision to follow Christ and beginning to set new cycles in motion. History does not have to repeat itself. It almost sounds like the dilemma of the apostle Paul in Romans 7 when he says when I want to do good, evil is present with me.

> *"For the good that I would I do not: but the evil which I would not, that I do."* (Rom. 7:19 KJV)

At first glance it appears that what the apostle Paul was trying to say is that this is the struggle of the Christian walk. One would almost think that the Christian walk is a roller coaster ride of ups and downs, failures and successes and repetitive cycles of failure. However, upon closer examination what we find is that the apostle Paul was saying that this is the dilemma of the person who is still under the old covenant system. His desperate cry is much like that of Solomon when he says, "Who shall deliver me from the body of this death?" (Rom. 7:24). Am I doomed to repeat my same failures over and over again? Does history have to repeat itself? Then the powerful answer comes to the question of, who shall deliver me. Thank God, He will! Yes, something can break the cycles of failure. There is something new. There is a brand new covenant where God writes His law upon our hearts. There is a new creature and a new man. There is a new nature. His mercy is new every morning. He will give us a new heart and a new spirit. We will speak with new tongues. There is a new heaven and a new earth. There is a new song and a New Jerusalem. There is new wine, not in old bottles; for you cannot put the new wine of the new covenant into the old bottles of the old covenant. There is a new garment, not a patched up old covenant garment. There is a new name and, last but not least, Revelation 21 makes this declaration, "Behold I make all things new!" Solomon, under an old covenant, locked into repetitive behavior was desperate for something new. But thanks be to God who always causes us to triumph. He has made everything new. We are not destined to the roller coaster ride of failure and frustration. We are called to a life of victory. We have entered into the new country of grace — a new life in a new land! We now live at Graceland and Adam has left the building!

The New Land is a Life in Christ

In the old covenant the Promised Land was a piece of real estate. In the new covenant, according to Hebrews 4, the Promised Land is rest in the finished work of Christ.

> *"Let us therefore fear, lest, a promise being left us of entering into his rest, any of you should seem to come short of it. For unto us was the gospel preached, as well as unto them: but the word preached did not profit them, not being mixed with faith in them that heard it. For we which have believed do enter into rest, as he said, As I have sworn in my wrath, if they shall enter into my rest: although the works were finished from the foundation of the world."* (Heb. 4:1-3 KJV)

By faith we entered this new life in a new land. Our water baptism is a powerful picture of crossing the Jordan River and entering into the Promised Land with our heavenly Joshua leading the way. This new land called rest does not make us spiritual couch potatoes. It simply declares that everything that I do from here on out must flow from rest. It is living in houses that I did not build and eating from vineyards that I did not plant. It is simply learning to live out of the finished work of Christ. I am no longer working to get salvation. I am working out of salvation. I am not doing to be. I already be, so I do. This country is a heavenly country. I believe it is the same one that the men of faith in Hebrews 11 looked for. This heavenly country is not only in my future, it is available right now by faith.

> *"And **hath** raised us up together, and made us sit together in heavenly places in Christ Jesus:"* (Eph. 2:6 KJV)

The location of this new heavenly land is in Christ. Please note that the word hath denotes not something in our future, but something in our past readily available to be enjoyed right now. It is far above all principalities and powers, might and dominions. When you get in this new land called Christ, milk and honey will flow from your life.

> *"Blessed be the God and Father of our Lord Jesus Christ, who **hath** blessed us with all spiritual blessings in heavenly places in Christ:"* (Eph. 1:3 KJV)

This verse tells us how we got in this heavenly land. It is interesting to me that the word blessing in this text is the Greek word eulogia. An English word we derive from this Greek word is eulogy. A eulogy is something you say over somebody that is dead. Are you ready to be blessed? Here it is then, "You are dead and your life is hid with Christ in God". When you went down into the watery grave of water baptism and identified with the work of the cross, God made a pronunciation of death over who you were in Adam. It was at that same moment that He placed you in the heavenly Christ Jesus. The heavenly is a life in Christ. Let me say it another way. You are already where a lot of folks are dying to be. You have died and gone to heaven. You are dead and your life is hid with Christ in God. Therefore, as a citizen of heaven you have certain rights and privileges. Let us not live like strangers right in the land of promise, but let us enjoy the benefits of a life in Christ now. The moment you were born again you were translated out of the kingdom of darkness and into the kingdom of his dear Son. I am not saying that there is not a heaven in your future. I am simply saying you don't have to wait until you die physically to enjoy the benefits of being a kingdom citizen.

MARRIED TO ANOTHER

> *"Never again will you be called 'The Forsaken City' or 'The Desolate Land.' Your new name will be 'The City of God's Delight' and 'The Bride of God,' for the LORD delights in you and will claim you as his bride."* (Isa. 62:4 NLT)

The benefits of a life in Christ are the benefits of the married life. With all the blessings and benefits of our union with Christ we no longer fall into the pit of the harlot system that says, "I sit as Queen and I am not a widow" (Rev.18:7). But we have learned how our old man, our first husband Adam, came to an end. We have put off the old man with its former lifestyle. I am no longer oppressed by a withered hand that keeps putting me back in Adam and handing me a cup of suffering that is no longer mine in which to partake. The only cup I am partaking of is the cup of the new covenant, and it is not a cup of suffering. It is the cup of blessing and favor. The new covenant is my marriage contract. It is what gives me the right to be intimate with Him. I am not going to get married to Him. I am already married to Him. If I am not married to Him already, it is not legal to be intimate with Him and it is illegal to use His name. The old covenant was the marriage certificate that kept me bound to Adam. Let's look at this scripture.

> *"Know ye not, brethren, (for I speak to them that know the law,) how that the law hath dominion over a man as long as he liveth? For the woman which hath an husband is bound by the law to her husband so long as he liveth; but if the husband be dead, she is loosed from the law of her husband. So then if, while her husband liveth, she be married to another man, she shall be called an adulteress: but if her husband be dead, she is free from that law; so that she is no adulteress, though she be married to another man. Wherefore, my brethren, ye also are become dead to the law by the body of Christ; that ye should be married to another, even to him who is raised from the dead, that we should bring forth fruit unto God." (Rom. 7:1-4 KJV)*

The law of the old covenant is what kept us bound to a marriage with Adam. As long as our first husband Adam was alive we were bound by the law to that husband. But now that our first husband Adam is dead we are free to be married to another, even to Him who was raised from the dead. The whole sixth chapter of the book of Romans tells you how the old man was removed. It is about reckoning how this occurred. By the time you get to this chapter you should have an understanding that you are dead to the law and dead to sin by the body of Christ and that you should be married to another even to Him who is raised from the dead. This text is not dealing with divorce and remarriage in the natural. Primarily it is dealing with a far more spiritual revelation. He's talking about being married to Adam or to Christ. It is very clear in this text the second husband is Christ. And very clearly He must know that your first husband Adam is dead or He would not have married you. Because according to this text if your first husband Adam is still alive, then Christ would be in adultery by marrying you. It is clear then from this text that Adam is dead. You buried him in baptism. You are free to be married to another and to enjoy all the benefits of marriage especially bringing forth fruit unto God. Please do not carry the baggage of your first marriage into this new relationship with Christ. Clean out the entire residue of Adam's belongings out of your closet. Take his picture down off the wall and get rid of all the traces of that old life and enjoy your new life in Christ.

You may ask the question when did this marriage occur? I think it began at the cross. A couple of things are happening that confirm that this marriage took place at the cross. In the garden when God brought the woman to the man He said to him, "For this cause will a man leave his father and mother and cleave to his wife". When Jesus is hanging on the cross He looks down from the cross and sees His mother weeping. He addresses her not by using a term of endearment. He does not call her mama. Instead He uses a prophetic term. He calls her woman. First I think He is trying to give His mother some comfort as she is deeply distressed watching her son die. He was trying to remind her of an ancient prophecy that said the seed of the woman will bruise the head of the serpent. When He calls her woman He is trying to shock her mind to get her to understand that she in fact was the woman, and he was the one who was about to bruise the head of the serpent. He then says to John, "Son, behold your mother". He says to His mother, "Woman, behold your son". He is giving His mother into the care of John. A few moments later He will cry, "My God my God why have you forsaken me?" What is occurring here is that He is leaving His father and His mother and He is cleaving to His bride.

Secondly, I know it took place at the cross because it was the place where my first husband Adam died, and the marriage contract of the law that had me bound to Him was nailed. The death of Christ got rid of my old husband and the resurrection of Christ gave birth to my new Husband. I do not think it is an accident that the first Adam in an ancient garden was put into a deep sleep and his side was opened and a rib was taken from his side to bring forth a bride. The last Adam was about to have the spear of a Roman soldier pierce His side out of which would flow blood and water that would bring forth His bride without spot or wrinkle.

> *"Husbands, love your wives, even as Christ also loved the church, and gave himself for it; That he might sanctify and cleanse it with the washing of water by the word, That he might present it to himself a glorious church, not having spot, or wrinkle, or any such thing; but that it should be holy and without blemish."* (Eph. 5:25-27 KJV)

Most of us have been taught all of our life that this is something that God is going to do in the future. We have been told that Jesus is coming back for a church not having spot, wrinkle, blemish or any such thing. However, that is not what this scripture is saying. The problem with that thinking is that it keeps us from enjoying the benefits of being married to Him right now and postpones it to some distant future. This scripture says Christ loved the church and gave Himself for it. He gave himself at the cross and the blood and the water that flowed from His side was enough to purge and cleanse any spot that I might have. You may not think that I look like I don't have any spots. But He did not present me to you as not having spot. He presented me to Himself not having spot, wrinkle, blemish or any such thing. He sees me as spotless because He knows how I was made clean. He is fully aware that the agency of the blood and the water that flowed from His side was enough to cleanse the vilest sinner. Look at the words that the king utters to his bride in the Song of Solomon. Is it not a picture of how our heavenly King Jesus sees His bride?

> *"Until the day break, and the shadows flee away, I will get me to the mountain of myrrh, and to the hill of frankincense. Thou art all fair, my love; **there is no spot in thee.**"* (Song 4:6-7 KJV)

In this text the mountain of myrrh speaks of the place of His suffering. It points us to Calvary where Jesus suffered and died. It was at this place that He presented us to Himself not having spot, wrinkle, blemish or any such thing. When the Lord first opened this scripture to me I said to Him, "I don't believe that", to which he replied, "I know you don't believe it. That's why you're acting like you have spots." When we truly believe what He said about us is true it will change our behavior. We will know the truth and the truth will make us free. We will walk by faith and not by sight. I think one of the biggest reasons why folks do not draw near to God is because we are always pointing out their faults. They never feel holy enough or good enough to stand in His presence. It would be like seeing your bride as she presents herself to you on your wedding night and all you can do is point out the blemish on her face, the spot on her dress or saying, "Your breath sure does stink". Do you think she will feel like being intimate with you? I doubt it! But that is what we have done to the church, the bride of Christ. We continue to point out her failures and spots and wonder why she never gives herself to Him completely. That is what I believe is represented by this restored withered hand. It is not balled up like a fist to strike you. It is stretched forth from the posture of rest to encourage you to draw near with a true heart in full assurance of faith. It is stretched out to sheep that had fallen into a pit. It is reaching out to them with an outstretched hand of grace and mercy. It is the hand of provision that reveals to them the goodness of God. It is from this viewpoint that we enable people to bring forth fruit unto God.

Healing the Hand

I think that one of the great tragedies of this day is that we have never allowed people to see the outstretched hand of grace and mercy that flows from the unforced rhythm of grace. We have shown them the balled up fist or a backhand that flows from domination and fear. We have shown them the old covenant hand that will not allow people to see the goodness of God that leads them to repentance. Let's look at this scripture.

> *"And the* LORD *said unto Moses, I will do this thing also that thou hast spoken: for thou hast found grace in my sight, and I know thee by name. And he said, I beseech thee, shew me thy glory. And he said, I will make all my goodness pass before thee, and I will proclaim the name of the* LORD *before thee; and will be gracious to whom I will be gracious, and will shew mercy on whom I will shew mercy. And he said, Thou canst not see my face: for there shall no man see me, and live. And the* LORD *said, Behold, there is a place by me, and thou shalt stand upon a rock: And it shall come to pass, while my glory passeth by, that I will put thee in a cleft of the rock, and will cover thee with my hand while I pass by: And I will take away mine hand, and thou shalt see my back parts: but my face shall not be seen."* (Ex. 33:17-23 KJV)

Moses, who was the faithful mediator of the old covenant, only ever asked God for two things. Let me see your glory and show me the Promised Land. He died short of both of those. The closest he comes is in this text. God said I'm going to hide you in the cleft of the rock and I'm going to allow all my goodness to pass before you and then I am going to place my hand over the rock and after I pass by I will remove my hand and you will not be allowed to see my face only my hinder parts. To me this powerfully speaks of what occurs when we have five-fold ministries with an old covenant mentality that will not allow you to see the goodness of God or the face of God. They put their hand over your face and only allow you to see His hinder parts. Because to them God is always turning His back on you and walking away. But that is an old covenant concept of God. In the new covenant God will never turn His back on you. For in Him there is neither variableness nor turning of shadows. He will never turn His back on you. He will never leave you nor forsake you. I always thought that it was unfair that Moses, who was the mediator of that old covenant, never got to enter the Promised Land. I always thought if Moses didn't make it, then I don't have a chance. Then I realized that what God was trying to show me through this story was that not even Moses the mediator of that covenant made it by the works of the law. God was trying to show us that it is only by the hearing of faith, because the law concludes all under sin so that He can have mercy on all. Under the law there is none righteous, no not even one. If Moses would have made it we would have been forever destined to do it by works instead of by grace.

Oh, but wait! 1500 years later the two prayer requests of Moses are ringing throughout the corridors of glory and they are haunting God. On a mountain called Transfiguration Moses reenters the theater of human expression along with Elijah (Matt 17:1-7). They represent the law and the prophets. It is on that mountain that God answers the prayer request of Moses, "Let me see your glory". As he gazes into the face of Jesus Christ he realizes that glory is not smoke in a corner, but it is found in the face of Jesus Christ. Notice, this time he did not see God's hinder parts. He looks right in the face of Jesus Christ, and while he is looking in the face of Jesus he realizes that the Promised Land is not a place but a person. This time he looked into the face of God and lived. He saw the goodness of God wrapped in human flesh standing in front of him. When you enter into Christ who is our Promised Land you enter into His rest and have ceased from your own labor. Christ is our Promised Land because He is the fulfillment of all the promises that God made to the fathers. In Hebrews four we enter into His rest and once again that rest is our Promised Land. It is from this wonderful Promised Land called Christ and His rest that there is an outflow of milk and honey. All of

The Body of Moses

I think it is interesting to note that in the Old Testament the Bible said that God buried Moses in a place where nobody knows where he is to this day (Deut. 34:6). It also says in Jude 1:9 that Michael disputed with the devil for the body of Moses. When I think about the body of Moses I think about it as representing not just one man, but the whole body of the law of the Mosaic system. I believe that if the devil could have gotten the body of Moses he would have forever used it against us as a tool of condemnation. Colossians 2 tells us that the weapon of our enemy is the handwriting of ordnance that was against us. It was the Law of Moses. But now no weapon formed against us can prosper, and any tongue that rises up against us in condemnation will utterly be condemned because our righteousness is of the Lord. Sad to say, but many ministries put the weapon right back in the enemy's hands when they preach the law and put us under condemnation. They put the withered hand of old covenant ministry over our faces, never allowing us to see the goodness of God that leads to repentance.

I was driving to Cincinnati, Ohio, many years ago and you may think I'm crazy but the Lord told me where Moses was buried. He told me he was buried the same place that I was buried, in the tomb of Joseph of Arimathea. Not only were we crucified with Christ, we were buried with Him. If you cannot find Moses, then you cannot find me. So stop being on a sin hunt. Stop looking for your old man because he is dead and hid with Christ in God!

The whole message of what is occurring here on the Mount of Transfiguration is a powerful picture of being redeemed from the curse of the law. Even the men that are with Him and the meaning of their names are significant. He took with him Peter whose name means stone, James whose name means to replace and John whose name means love. Because what was taking place on the Mount of Transfiguration is that the stone (Peter) of the law was being replaced (James) with love (John). Peter, with all of his zeal, says let us build here three tabernacles; one for Jesus, one for Moses and one for Elijah. In other words, let's make this Jesus plus the law and the prophets. Immediately the Father's voice interrupted like thunder and said, "This is my beloved Son, hear ye Him!" In other words, it is Jesus plus nothing! I think it to be of great importance what were the first words out of the mouth of Jesus; especially since the Father said this is my Son, hear Him. His first words to fearful apostles who were expecting to drop dead because they had just seen God and lived was, "Fear not". Under the old covenant there was an expectation of death once you looked into the face of God. But now in the new covenant we no longer have to fear. For then we looked through a glass darkly, but now we can see face to face. God is now saying to all valid five-fold ministries everywhere, "Remove your hand from covering my goodness, stand forth from the position of the Sabbath rest and stretch forth your hand to sheep that are in the pit and lift them out". It is time to declare the goodness and the grace of God! Let's take a look at this hand in the book of Revelation.

The Hand from the Sabbath

"I John, who also am your brother, and companion in tribulation, and in the kingdom and patience of Jesus Christ, was in the isle that is called Patmos, for the word of God, and for the testimony of Jesus Christ. I was in the Spirit on the Lord's day, and heard behind me a great voice, as of a trumpet, Saying, I am Alpha and Omega, the first and the last:" (Rev. 1:9-11 KJV)

In this text the apostle John is on an island called Patmos. He is there on the Lord's Day. The Lord's Day is the Sabbath. It is also a term that is used for the Day of Atonement which was in the Sabbath month. You decide which fits here because both speak of rest. Of course, it is the atoning work of Jesus that brings us into the Sabbath rest. It is His finished work. Everything John is about to describe is from the perspective of the finished work. He hears a voice like a trumpet. This trumpet is not a fat baby with wings that will step out of the cloud. It is the ram's horn that was used to announce the Day of Atonement and various other Sabbath activities and feasts. It is also important to note that the ram's horn comes from the death of a male lamb. Of course, we know that the Lamb slain was Jesus Christ. So what John is hearing is a message declaring what the death of this Lamb has produced. The word Patmos literally means "my killing".[1] He is there for the testimony of Jesus Christ. The word testimony in Strong's concordance is from a word meaning martyr. So he is on an island called Patmos to get an understanding of the martyrdom of Jesus. As he gets a revelation of the death of Christ and His finished work, it brings him into a Sabbath understanding. He hears the message coming from the ram's horn and it is coming from behind him. It is from this clear sounding word coming through the death of a male lamb that he realizes that his Patmos, literally his killing, is not in front of him but behind him. I think the greatest revelation that will come to the church is not a revelation of what God is going to do, but it is a revelation of what He's already done at the cross. You are not dying. You are dead and your life is hid with Christ in God. The voice from the trumpet says I am Alpha and Omega, the first and the last. I think what He is simply saying here is that I identified with you in the Alpha Son. I became what you were in the first Adam and I took you to the cross. Through my death burial and resurrection I became the last Adam the Omega Son. You see the message that is coming forth from this Sabbath rest is not a message of trying to kill the old man. Jesus already took care of that at the cross. Even when you make mistakes it is not your old man being resurrected. It is an immature new man who is not fully developed yet. It amazes me how many people believe in the resurrection of the old man more than they believe in the resurrection of the new man. Many times well-meaning preachers are much like the Roman soldiers that were coming to break the legs of Jesus as He hung on the cross, because it was not lawful to be on the cross on the Sabbath day. What we must discover is that we no longer need to break the legs of people in our churches to try to expedite their death, because we will discover as we gaze steadfastly at the cross that we are not dying, we are already dead. And it is illegal for anyone to be on the cross on the Sabbath day.

THE APOSTLE

In this first chapter of Revelation the seven messengers to the churches are in His right hand because they are the messengers that are being adjusted to declare the message of rest. They are the hand that is being restored on the Sabbath. It is not an accident that with the first church at Ephesus he begins to adjust the apostle (Rev.2). His message to this church is, you have those that say they are apostles and they are not they are liars. They have taught you works and labor and you did it for my namesake. In this church He says to remember where you fell from. He is not telling them to remember where they fell from last night. He is telling them to remember what caused the original fall. What caused the original fall was feeding from the tree of the knowledge of good and evil. We have stated in a previous chapter that this is a picture of the old covenant that was all about works and labor. He connects this church clear back to the Garden of Eden by telling them if you overcome I will give you to eat of the tree of life that is in the midst of the paradise of God. That tree of life is found on Golgotha's hill. When we feed from this tree we will cease from our labors because we have discovered how the work was finished. Oh that God would raise up true apostles that have more than just a title on a name card, but men of God who truly preach the death, burial and resurrection of Jesus Christ. Apostles that continue to lay the foundation like Paul determine to know nothing among you but Christ and Him crucified. These true apostles will restore us to our first love, no longer being motivated by a law, but by love.

THE PROPHET

To the church at Pergamos he begins to adjust a prophet named Balaam. What Balaam represents is a prophet for hire. He was hired to curse the people of God. He climbed the mountain in order to see the people of God from a higher perspective. When he did he beheld Israel in her tents (Num. 24:5-9). Anyone who has ever studied the Old Testament knows that when the camp was at rest the children of Israel were camped in the shape of a cross. When he saw them camped in the shape of a cross he began to prophesy that if God has blessed Jacob who can curse him. True New Testament prophets will bless and curse not (Rom. 12:14). The only way you can curse someone in the New Testament is to put them back up under the Law of Moses (Gal. 3:10). New Testament prophets will speak from a mercy seat and not a judgment seat. They will speak to your potential and not your problem. A New Testament prophet will mentor you while an Old Testament prophet will torment you. An Old Testament prophet will bring your sin to remembrance while a New Testament prophet will declare your righteousness. An Old Testament prophet will tear down while a New Testament prophet will build up. Remember on the Mount of Transfiguration Elijah appeared with Moses. Now I am not saying that the days of prophets are over. I am saying that the day of the old covenant prophet is over. Elijah must give way to Elisha. Elijah's name ends with JAH and it connects him with the old covenant Jehovah names of God and literally means my God He is Jehovah. Elisha's name ends with SHA and means God of salvation. The ministry of these two men powerfully typifies the two covenants. Elijah primarily is preoccupied with judgment and calling down fire from heaven and shutting up the heavens that there be no rain, etc. Elisha is primarily focused on filling the widow's oil and meal barrel, raising the dead, healing Naaman's leprosy and making ax heads float. His ministry is primarily focused on salvation or restoration. Let's look at this New Testament example where Jesus corrects His disciples for trying to act like Elijah.

> *"And they did not receive him, because his face was as though he would go to Jerusalem. And when his disciples James and John saw this, they said, Lord, wilt thou that we command fire to come down from heaven, and consume them, even as Elias did? But he turned, and rebuked them, and said, Ye know not what*

manner of spirit ye are of. For the Son of man is not come to destroy men's lives, but to save them. And they went to another village." (Luke 9:53-56 KJV)

The disciples of Jesus are acting with an old covenant mentality here. They want to act like Elijah. It would almost look like a noble thing to call down fire from heaven and destroy all those that don't seem to be receiving Him. However, Jesus says to His disciples you do not know what spirit you are of. I don't think He is accusing them of operating under the spirit of the devil. I think He is accusing them of operating under an old covenant spirit, the spirit of Elijah. It is at this point that He gives us a glimpse into the purpose and function of new covenant prophets. Jesus is the pattern for New Testament prophets. He says the Son of Man is not come to destroy men's lives but to save them! Sad to say, but many so-called prophets in this hour are still trying to call down fire from heaven. They will say things like, God is getting ready to destroy America, and that many of the catastrophes that we have suffered with hurricanes and terrorist attacks and oil spills are the judgment of God. They will continue to operate in the spirit of Elijah. But I beg to differ with those thoughts. I do not believe God is destroying America. I believe Americans are destroying America. God is standing with His hand outstretched saying I stand ready to be your Savior. Most of the things that we suffer in our lives are not a result of the judgment of God. They are the result of our stupidity. God doesn't have to judge us. Our own sin reproves us, and our own iniquity judges us when we receive the results of our actions. But Jesus came to save us from our sin. If you want to see how Jesus reacts to a typhoon or hurricane you must go back to the story of when the disciples were on the ship. The ship was being blown around by contrary winds. Jesus is asleep in the ship. He is in a posture of rest. When they awaken Him He does not come out on the front of the ship and say, "This is the judgment of God." or "This is an act of God." If you want to know what an act of God looks like, it is when Jesus, who has dominion and authority, operates as a Savior and speaks from the posture of rest to the wind and the sea and tells it to be calmed and be still. It is an act of God, when instead of prophesying judgment on nations like Haiti in the recent earthquake, we instead respond like saviors with food, clothing, shelter, spiritual impartation and other such acts of salvation. Perhaps it is time that we act like Jesus instead of Elijah and seek to save men's lives instead of destroy them. Perhaps it is time that we begin to exercise our New Testament redemptive dominion and begin to rebuke some of these catastrophes and earthquakes, etc.

DOUBLE PORTION

Remember the story of Elijah when he was about to be taken. He said to his servant Elisha to ask me for what you will. Then Elisha asked for a double portion. The double portion was the right of the firstborn son that was given to him by his father as an inheritance. Elijah said to him if you see me when I am taken you can have a double portion. Remember, on the Mount of Transfiguration it was really Jesus the firstborn son that saw Elijah taken, for he was swallowed up in Christ. And it was on that mountain that Jesus received the double portion or the right of the firstborn because He was the salvation of God. If you can truly see that the law and the prophets have been taken away and fulfilled in Christ you will receive a double portion anointing. It is the new anointing of the new covenant that flows from the Christ as the head, to His body. From that time forward the ministry of the prophet should not be one of judgment, but of restoration and salvation. Is it possible that later on in the book of Acts when the disciples saw Jesus taken up in the cloud that He released His mantle to us, His disciples, and said greater works than these shall you do because I go to the Father? His mantle of restoration and salvation now flows from the head to His body. There is a new breed of prophet on the scene today. It is a New Testament prophet with a more sure word of prophecy. That more sure word of prophecy is the testimony of Jesus Christ and His finished work. Old Testament prophets said He is coming and this is what He will do. New Testament prophets say He has come and this is what He has done.

The Evangelist

The word evangelist is only mentioned just a few times in the New Testament and is probably the least mentioned of the entire five-fold ministry. It is not mentioned at all in any of the seven churches in Revelation. However, that does not mean that we should minimize their importance. As a matter of fact, I believe God is raising up a new breed of evangelists. The word evangelist is a Greek word that simply means to proclaim glad tidings or good news to preach the Gospel. Perhaps we should all become evangelists, or should I say preachers of good news. Most of the so-called evangelists that I grew up around did not preach good news. They would tell us how bad we were, and what all was wrong with us. They would tell us how angry God was and how doomed we were. We were sinners in the hands of an angry God. They would talk of horrible world events and scare people to altars. They would dangle us over hell every week and tell us that we were going to bust it wide open.

They would leave there and brag about how many people got saved in their meetings, but would fail to tell you that they are the same people that get saved every time they have a revival. The evangelist would talk them out of their salvation and preach the law and shut up their faith until they became unbelievers. And while I do believe that we need genuine altar services, sometimes it's just as successful if you have folk who are strong enough believers not to constantly feel like they are undone or have to go back to the altar again. You can only stay on that religious treadmill so long until you become so discouraged you throw in the towel and quit. They did have some limited success preaching the bad news and fear. The only problem with getting people to the altars through fear is that you have to continually keep them fearful to keep them in the house of God. I am concerned that many people do not love God. They just don't like the alternative. They feel like they have been held hostage by an abusive father. The problem is that the thing you fear, you mostly come to hate. Someone might argue that the fear of the Lord is the beginning of wisdom. Then I would reply that is an Old Testament concept. In the New Testament Christ is the wisdom of God and the power of God. And when you meet Him, perfect love casts out all the fear.

"For God hath not given us the spirit of fear; but of power, and of love, and of a sound mind." (2 Tim. 1:7 KJV)

Let us compare two scriptures to show you how Jesus defines the word fear in the New Testament.

*"Then saith Jesus unto him, Get thee hence, Satan: for it is written, Thou shalt **worship** the Lord thy God, and him only shalt thou serve."* (Matt. 4:10 KJV)

*"Thou shalt **fear** the LORD thy God, and serve him, and shalt swear by his name."* (Deut. 6:13 KJV)

In Matthew 4:10 Jesus is quoting Deuteronomy 6:13 and He exchanges the word fear for the word worship. I believe that when we preach the good news of the Gospel it will make people fall in love with Jesus all over again. It will make them stand in awe of God where they cannot help but worship such an awesome God. Romans chapter 2 says it is the goodness of God that leads men to repentance. When we preach the goodness of God I believe people will flock to Him by the multitudes. Love is a much more powerful force than fear. If people would ever walk down a church aisle and give their hearts to God because they have fallen in love with Him, a team of wild horses could not keep them from faithfully attending His house or serving Him. They would give offerings not because they were afraid God was going to curse them, but because they love Him. I believe people do not attend church because they cannot take the continual threats and bad news that makes them fearful. We have what I call an abused spouse syndrome in the church in America. We take our beating because we believe they love us and somehow we deserve it. My advice is run for your life! What part of "good news" don't we understand? God is restoring the withered hand and the evangelist is one of the digits in that hand. A new model of evangelism is beginning to emerge and I am praying that God will raise up true evangelists that will proclaim the Good News in this hour.

The Pastor

All seven of the messages to the church in the first couple of chapters of revelation are written to the angel of the church. Some translate the word angel as pastor so that all of these messages are first sent to the pastor of the church. I have already written one volume on the first several chapters of the book of Revelation. It is available by this author so I will not go into great depth in dealing with all of the adjustments that are made.[2] I will, however, tell you that everything He promises the ones who overcome is contingent upon them repenting. The Greek word for repent literally means to change your mind. Most of the adjustments being made in the first couple of chapters of Revelation are designed to change our minds from an old covenant mentality to a new covenant mentality. And the promises made to them that overcome are the blessings of the new covenant. The church at Ephesus must move away from work and labor. If they do they will receive the tree of life. The church at Smyrna must move away from a suffering mentality and if they do they will receive the crown of life. The church at Pergamos must move away from prophets who curse the people of God. If they do they will receive hidden manna, a white stone and a new name. The church at Sardis had a reputation of being alive, but they were really dead and had defiled garments. He promises them white raiment which speaks of the righteousness given to us as a gift in the new covenant, and our name in the book of life. He promises the church at Philadelphia, a church of brotherly love, that they will become the temple of God and the city of God which is New Jerusalem. He also says that He will write upon him his new name which speaks of his new nature. The church at Laodicea must repent of their lukewarm attitudes, their blindness and their attitude of thinking they were rich; when in reality there was a real spiritual poverty being uncovered. He promises them that He would sup with him and bring them to the table of the Lord which is a picture of communion in the New Testament. He will give them the right to sit with Him in His throne and have authority to operate and act as kings and priests; teaching them to function not in an Old Testament form of governing but in a New Testament form of government called the Kingdom of God. This throne is not a judgment seat. It is a mercy seat and all ministry must flow from the mercy seat.

> *"Woe be unto the pastors that destroy and scatter the sheep of my pasture! saith the LORD. Therefore thus saith the LORD God of Israel against the pastors that feed my people; Ye have scattered my flock, and driven them away, and have not visited them: behold, I will visit upon you the evil of your doings, saith the LORD. And I will gather the remnant of my flock out of all countries whither I have driven them, and will bring them again to their folds;* **and they shall be fruitful and increase.** *And I will set up shepherds over them which shall feed them:* **and they shall fear no more, nor be dismayed, neither shall they be lacking, saith the LORD.***" (Jer. 23:1-4 KJV)

THE TEACHER

And last, but not least, is the teacher. The teacher is addressed at the church at Thyatira because they are allowing the woman Jezebel to teach and seduce my servants to commit fornication and to eat things offered to idols. Fornication is defined as intimate sexual relationship outside of marriage. I have already showed you in previous chapters that the new covenant is your marriage certificate. Therefore, it is legal for you to be intimate with Jesus. Because I am married to Him I should take my commitment very serious and not compromise my covenant with Him by eating things offered to idols or committing adultery with other gods. What agreement does the temple of God have with idols? What I think this means is not just eating a piece of beef that was offered to some false statue or image. I think it means when we feed on concepts about God that are not true we are feeding on idols' meat. These false images are in the chambers of our image-a-nation between our ears. When we have images of ourselves that are contrary to how God views us, that also is an idol. Tragically enough we bow our knee to these false images and we serve them. I believe true teachers are coming on the scene that will hold before us a view of God that will change us. You will become what you behold. Look at the Scripture.

> *"And as we have borne the image of the earthy, we shall also bear the image of the heavenly."* (I Cor. 15:49 KJV)

When we teach people who they are in Adam it should not surprise us when they bear the image of the earthy. What we must do is hold the mirror of the Word of God before them and continually tell them who they are in Christ. Because of His finished work it will cause them to truly bear the image of the heavenly.

> *"But their minds were blinded: for until this day remaineth the same vail untaken away in the reading of the Old Testament; which vail is done away in Christ. But even unto this day, when Moses is read, the vail is upon their heart. Nevertheless when it shall turn to the Lord, the vail shall be taken away. Now the Lord is that Spirit: and where the Spirit of the Lord is, there is liberty. But we all, with open face beholding as in a glass the glory of the Lord, are changed into the same image from glory to glory, even as by the Spirit of the Lord."* (2 Cor. 3:14-18 KJV)

True new covenant teachers are coming on the scene that are not teaching us the letter of the law. They are not putting a veil over our face so that we cannot see who we are in Christ. They are able ministers of the new covenant, not of the letter that kills, but the Spirit that gives life.

The promise that God makes to the church at Thyatira if they keep His works till the end is that He will give them power over the nations and they will break them in pieces like the vessels of a potter. Perhaps these nations are not only literal nations like the United States. Perhaps they are nations like Imagi-Nation, Condem-Nation, Denomi-Nation, etc. It is these nations that must be shattered like a potter's vessel. Perhaps that is the work of this smallest finger on the hand, the teacher. Can you hear the Lord saying to this man with the withered hand "Stand forth and stretch out your hand from the Sabbath day from the posture of rest and get the sheep out of the pit?" With this hand now adjusted, let's see how it affected John the revelator in Revelation 1.

> *"And when I saw him, I fell at his feet as dead. And he laid his right hand upon me, saying unto me, Fear not; I am the first and the last:"* (Rev. 1:17 KJV)

When you truly see Him as John saw Him. You will see Him as the first and the last. Remember what I have written in this chapter a few pages ago when I told you He identified with you in the first Adam, and through His death burial and resurrection He became the last Adam. He was God's method of getting rid of who you were in Adam. You were crucified with Christ. That should make you fall at His feet as a dead man. It should bring you into a perpetual Sabbath; not trying to kill the old Adam nature or trying to modify the behavior of the old man because you have reckoned him to be dead. Remember, John is seeing this vision from the viewpoint of the day of the Lord or the Sabbath. He hears a voice behind him and he realizes his killing is not in his future, it is in his past. It is at this point that He lays His right hand on him. Not the balled fist or the backhand of religion, but an outstretched hand that is no longer withered and imparts resurrection life to him and releases him from all fear. He then tells him to take the message which he has seen and heard and send it to the churches.

Do you hear the trumpet calling you man and woman of God? It is calling you to stand forth and stretch out your hand to a dying creation. I believe it is time to change the way we do ministry. God wants to lay His hand of five-fold ministry, those who have an understanding of rest and the finished work, on sheep in the pit of religion and lift them out. Stretch forth your hand and minister from the unforced rhythm of grace!

ENDNOTES

1. J. B. Jackson, *A Dictionary of Scripture Proper Names,* 3rd edition (Loizeaux Brothers, Neptune, NJ. 1957) Pg. 73.

2. Dr. Lynn Hiles, *The Revelation Of Jesus Christ* (Destiny Image Publishers, Shippensburg, PA. 2007)

Chapter Four

A Woman Bowed
to the Earth

*"And he was **teaching** in one of the synagogues on the Sabbath. And, behold, there was a woman which had a spirit of infirmity eighteen years, and was bowed together, and could in no wise lift up herself. And when Jesus saw her, he called her to him, and said unto her, Woman, thou **art** loosed from thine infirmity. And he laid his hands on her: and immediately she was made straight, and glorified God. And the ruler of the synagogue answered with indignation, because that Jesus had healed on the sabbath day, and said unto the people, There are six days in which men ought to work: in them therefore come and be healed, and not on the sabbath day. The Lord then answered him, and said, Thou hypocrite, doth not each one of you on the Sabbath loose his ox or his ass from the stall, and lead him away to watering? And ought not this woman, being a daughter of Abraham, whom Satan hath bound, lo, these eighteen years, be loosed from this **bond** on the Sabbath day? And when he had said these things, all his adversaries were ashamed: and all the people rejoiced for all the glorious things that were done by him."* (Luke 13:10-17 KJV)

I think by now we have probably established the fact that the woman in the scripture can picture the church. This woman that was bowed to the earth is a powerful picture of the church today that has been bowed over and can no longer lift up her head. The New Testament word from Strong's for the word infirmity is feebleness of the mind or body by implication, a malady, morally or frailty. Disease, infirmity, sickness and weakness are all words that are translated from this word infirmity. It is clear that this pictures the condition of the church before she comes into a Sabbath rest. She is full of weakness, moral failure, sickness, disease and all kinds of things that we still see prevalent in the church today when the focus is not on the heavenly, but on the earthy. She is facing the earth and all she has ever been taught is who she is in Adam instead of who she is in Christ. Her focus is in the wrong place. All she ever heard was how bad it is on the earth, how big the devil is and how rotten she was. She was always made to face the dust of Adam's fallen state. She was a victim of identity theft.

I think it is important to note at this point that she was in this condition for 18 years. That number is significant in the scriptures because if you count it 6 + 6 + 6, it is the number of the beast. Eighteen in the scripture denotes bondage.[1] If we continue to keep the church under the law and keep them faced towards the realm of the earthy and who they are in Adam, they will continue to be in bondage; not only bondage to sin but religious bondage, and Jesus has come on this Sabbath day to set us free from this bondage. One of the things that I discovered in my study was that in the scriptures all of the words have a numerical value. It would be as if an A is worth 5, B is worth 10 or C is worth 20. All of the Greek letters in the alphabet have numerical value. When the number of the beast was written in the 13th chapter of Revelation, it was not written with Greek numbers. It was written with Greek letters that had the numerical value of six-hundred sixty-six. When I began to discover that, I started to do some research and found out that there are only five words in the entire New Testament that have a numerical value of 666. The second word I came across was the word tradition.[2] Interestingly enough it is used 13 times. Each time the word is used where Jesus would say to the people, "You have by your traditions, made the word of God ineffective or powerless." I believe that is what this woman is struggling with; powerlessness and weakness, an infirmity that is a result of being under tradition for many years. While many people are waiting on the mark of the beast to come to the grocery store or the credit card or some other kind of thing that would be stamped on their hand, perhaps we need to take a look at the traditions in the church that have made the word of God ineffective. Sometimes I think we are pro-God, but anti-Christ. For a more in-depth study of the rest of the words that have a numerical value of 666 I recommended that you order this author's book, titled God's Beauty and the Beast. Such are many religions throughout the world, no matter what religion it is; whether it is Christianity or Buddhism or Islam. If they are pro-God and anti-Christ, they still are void of the life of Christ that can lift us up out of the realm of the dust and look at who we are in the heavens. Our problem is that we have always allowed tradition to dictate the same old things to us and we repeat it over and over and over again. Jesus comes to this woman in this condition who could in no way lift up herself. All of her self-help performance-based efforts did not work. All of the religious formulas had failed. He began to say to her, "Woman, thou are loosed from thine infirmity." He laid his hands on her. Perhaps the hands He laid on her could be identified with what I wrote in the last chapter. There is a pair of hands coming forth from the perspective of the Sabbath that are no longer withered. They are going to be released and turned loose on this woman who is bowed to the earth. They are ministry that is flowing from a totally different viewpoint and a different perspective than the law of the old covenant. They are coming from a voice that is speaking from the heavens.

The Bible says that when He laid his hands on her, she was made straight immediately and glorified God. The response that immediately came from the religious rulers that had perpetuated this kind of tradition upon her answered Him with indignation and was upset; not because the woman was healed, but because he had done it on the Sabbath day. Jesus had broken their religious traditions. Isn't it amazing that almost every miracle that Jesus does throughout the scriptures, He has to almost, as it were in their eyes, break the law in order to do it. To them, He broke the law of the Mosaic system when He would heal a woman who was bowed to the earth on the Sabbath, or He would touch a man with leprosy, or He would heal a woman with an issue of blood. Even that is an example of what the law said was not supposed to occur. A woman that was bleeding was not, under the Law of Moses, supposed to touch a man because when she touched him, he would become unclean by reason of her uncleanness. In the New Testament Jesus became unclean by reason of her uncleanness. She became clean by reason of His cleanness. In other words, an incredible exchange took place there and she took His cleanness and He took her sin. He took her uncleanness. He was made to be sin and she was made righteous. In the eyes of tradition, He broke their law.

THE MAN IN THE MIRROR

The response that Jesus had to their traditions that kept this woman bound to her infirmity was, "Does not each one of you on the Sabbath day loose his ox or his ass from the stall and lead him away to watering?" Now I think it is important that He leads them to the water. Have you ever walked up to a pool of water and looked into it. Even if you are bowed down, what happens is that when you look into the water you see your reflection. You not only see your reflection, you see the heavenlies above you. What was taking place was that Jesus was bringing this woman to the water of the word and He was bringing her to the mirror of the word of God. It was the mirror that was no longer a glass darkly, but a mirror that had an open face so that you could steadfastly look into another image and the image you would see would be the image of the glory of God.

The Bible says that we are changed into the same image from glory to glory. We are not changed from heartache to heartache, or from misery to misery, or from trouble to trouble. We are changed as we behold the glory of the Lord in the mirror. Let's look at James 1:21-25 KJV.

*Wherefore lay apart all filthiness and superfluity of naughtiness, and receive with meekness the engrafted word, which is able to **save** your souls. But be ye doers of the word, and not hearers only, deceiving your own selves. For if any be a hearer of the word, and not a doer, he is like unto a man beholding his natural face in a glass: For he beholdeth himself, and goeth his way, and straightway forgetteth what manner of man he was. But whoso looketh into the perfect law of liberty, and continueth therein, he being not a forgetful hearer, but a doer of the work, this man shall be blessed in his deed.*

In this chapter of the book of James the message is to empower you to lay apart all of the weaknesses of your flesh and all of the filthiness in order to become a doer of the Word and not a hearer only. The trouble is that when most people preach this, they use this as a tool to browbeat the people of God; telling them they must be a doer. But this scripture is not just putting pressure on you to perform. It is telling you how to become a doer of the word. It tells you that if you are going to be a hearer of the word and not a doer, it is because you have looked into a mirror or in a glass and beheld your natural face. Then you went your own way and forgot what manner of man you saw in the mirror. I believe again that the mirror is the word of God. The tragedy is when most of us look into the mirror we usually look to see what is wrong with us and to see how ugly we are, and we end up with a mistaken identity. But this man was beholding his natural face. It is interesting to note that the word natural face here in Strong's concordance is the Greek word Genesis and it literally means the face of his birth. Specifically I believe it means the face of his new birth. I think I can confirm that in the text of this scripture because it goes on to say that whoever looks into the perfect law of liberty and continues in it, or in other words, does not forget his new identity, becomes a doer of the word. So as he is looking into the mirror, he is to behold not who he is in Adam, but he is to behold who he is in Christ. He is to look not into the Law of Moses to disqualify himself, but he is to look into the perfect law of liberty and continue there. The only way you can continue to be a hearer of the word and not a doer is to look into this mirror and behold your fresh new identity and then forget what manner of man you are. Then go your way and forget who you are in the new creation.

You see, one of the first things Jesus does in response to the accusations of the Pharisees is He looks at them and says, "Ought not this woman, who is a daughter of Abraham, be loose from this infirmity?" He is bringing her back to her identity as a daughter of Abraham. He is telling them that she has a legal right to restoration because of who she is in the father of faith. I think so many times we wonder why people are still bound to their infirmities, weaknesses and moral failures. It is because we bring them into our services and continue to browbeat them and never minister anything to them that would create faith in their hearts that would lift them up out of it. What we simply do is continue to put them down and keep them faced toward the realm of the dust. We keep them bound by our traditions until they cannot help themselves except to do the things that they believe to be true about who they are in Adam. No wonder they are hearers of the word and not doers only. We must bring them to the perfect law of liberty. We must continue to bring them back to the water where they can see not only their reflection, but they can also see the reflection of heaven in the water as they gaze steadfastly into it. Perhaps that is what is pictured in the story of Gideon.

> "And the LORD said unto Gideon, The people are yet too many; bring them down unto the water, and I will try them for thee there: and it shall be, that of whom I say unto thee, This shall go with thee, the same shall go with thee; and of whomsoever I say unto thee, This shall not go with thee, the same shall not go. So he brought down the people unto the water: and the LORD said unto Gideon, Every one that lappeth of the water with his tongue, as a dog lappeth, him shalt thou set by himself; likewise every one that boweth down upon his knees to drink. And the number of them that lapped, putting their hand to their mouth, were three hundred men: but all the rest of the people bowed down upon their knees to drink water. And the LORD

said unto Gideon, By the three hundred men that lapped will I save you, and deliver the Midianites into thine hand: and let all the other people go every man unto his place." (Judg. 7:4-7 KJV)

God is able to save by many or by a few is the story conveyed in this passage. The remnant that God has chosen in this hour to defeat the enemies of His people will be those who are willing to be led to the water. He is looking for those who can drink water by putting their hand to their mouth. I believe the hand that He is speaking of in this passage is the hand that I wrote about in the previous chapter. It is the hand of five-fold ministry who are bringing the people to the water of the word to see the reflection of mighty men of valor. It is those who are drinking from the hand of ministry that point them to their new identity. Drinking water from this kind of a hand will produce mighty warriors able to conquer the armies of the enemy because they are constantly being told how powerful and how victorious of an overcoming people they truly are. Those who are being disqualified are those who are bowing down and drinking water like a dog. This hand of five-fold ministry that is flowing from rest will not bring you into a dog's identity. You are not a dog. You're not a failure. You are not a loser. Do not believe those lies and you will go forth and conquer the armies of the Midianites not armed with swords and spears, but with a trumpet, a pitcher and a lamp. Remember a ram's horn trumpet comes from the death of a male lamb and symbolizes the message of the finished work of the true Lamb of God. When that message comes forth long and loud it will break the outer pitcher of the earthen vessel and the true beauty and the light that is within us will begin to shine forth, terrifying the host of the enemy.

Go back to Genesis 1:2 when the earth was without form and void and darkness was upon the face of the great deep. The Spirit of God moved on the face of the waters. In other words, God began to lean over and put His reflection in the water. When God put His reflection in the water, all of a sudden things began to change from darkness to light. What happens later in Genesis 6 is that man began to multiply on the face of the earth and daughters were born unto them. They began to multiply, not on the face of the water. They didn't begin to multiply the image of God. They began to multiply on the face of the earth. They began to multiply the earth face. They began to reproduce giants. Some of these giants they face later on when they face Goliath and such. Then God repented that He had made man on the earth and it grieved Him at His heart. What He begins to declare is, "I will destroy man whom I have created from the face of the earth." So He is going to destroy them from their earth face. But in Genesis 6:8 it says, "But Noah found grace in the eyes of the Lord." Oh that we would look into the eyes of God and behold the grace. As we behold in God's eyes, the grace, we will see a reflection not of our fallen man of earth, but we will see our reflection in the glory of the face of Jesus Christ. And that will change us into the same image. God's method of destroying that man of earth was that He is going to turn on the waterworks. He is going to fill the earth with water. When God began to release the fountains of the great deep and the water began to come upon the face of the earth, all of a sudden, God placed them in an Ark and they were lifted up above the face of the earth. In Genesis 7:17, "And *the flood* was forty days upon the earth; and the waters increased, and bare up the ark, and it was lifted up above the earth." I believe that when God turns up the water, it lifts us up above the earthy. The water removes our earth face.

I think it would be important to note at this point that the Ark of Noah is a powerful picture of the redemptive work of Christ. He is our Ark of safety. He is our vehicle out of an old world dominated by sin, by the curse, by thorns and thistles. He is the vehicle that will carry us into a new world where the curse has been reversed. It is not an accident that the dimensions of the Ark are 30 cubits high, which is the number in the Bible for the blood of Christ. It is 50 cubits wide, which is the number of Pentecost, because it was 50 days after Passover that Pentecost fell. It was 300 cubits long, which is the number of divine completeness.[3] It is not an accident that this Ark has 3 stories. If I could say it like this: it has an Outer Court, a Holy place and a Most Holy Place. Or I could say it like this: it has Passover, Pentecost and the Feast of Tabernacles. All of those are pictures of the progression of redemption. It also was pitched within and without with pitch. It is extraordinary that the word pitch is the Hebrew word that we translate atonement. So it is the atoning blood of Jesus that seals out the world and seals us in unto the day of redemption. The Ark has only one door and His name is Jesus. He is the door. There is only one window above. And if you were to look out that window you would have to look up because it is a window above. You cannot continue to look bowed to the earth and see anything except the earthy. If we are going to look out the window, we must look up!

It is not an accident that this Ark takes off out of a world dominated by sin and by the curse and later on it lands on a mountain called Ararat. The word Ararat means "the curse is reversed".[4] It is also not an accident that there are two birds that fly out the window of this Ark. I may have mentioned it before, but in this text I think it is important to mention again. One of these birds flies all the way through the scripture and lands in the book of Revelation where Babylon has become the hold of every foul spirit and the cage of every unclean and hateful bird. But the dove only has to fly to the book of Matthew, where it finds Jesus, the real Ark, coming forth up out of the waters of Jordan, being pictured in water baptism.

I do not think it's an accident later on when Apostle Peter makes the statement that the Ark of Noah is a picture of water baptism. You ask, "What are you saying Brother Hiles?" I am trying to tell you that when you get in this Ark called Christ, God turns up the water. The water increases to lift you up above the earth face. It lifts you up above the earthy and the waters prevail. What happened is our flesh died in that water. When you go down into the waters of baptism, what you are saying is, "I have gone down into the judgment of God when I was buried with Him in baptism and now I have been raised up in the newness of life. This is not with an old face but with my face as a reflection of what I have seen in the water my new Genesis face. What I saw in the water was the face of God, because when God moved upon the face of the water His face was reflecting and heaven was being seen in the reflection of the water." As a matter of fact, every living substance was destroyed which was upon the face of the ground; both man and cattle and creeping things and the fowl of the heaven. They were destroyed from the earth and Noah only remained alive and they that were with him in the Ark when the waters prevailed upon the earth 150 days. I think that what we are seeing is the purpose of leading these oxen, and everything we are, to this water; because what happens is that we behold that by the water was the place where God removes my earth face.

It was not an accident when the dove landed on Jesus in the waters of Jordan. When He came straightway up out of the water, the Spirit of God descended upon Him like a dove. The dove is the symbol of the Holy Spirit. It is also the symbol of peace. When John sees this he knows that Jesus literally is the new world. He is God's olive branch. He is the olive branch of the new world that God held out toward all humanity with the gospel of peace. When I really get a revelation of what occurred in the death, burial and resurrection of Jesus Christ, I feel like Noah. I think it is interesting to note as well that Noah's name means "rest". Because when you come out of this boat into this new world and into this perpetual Sabbath day called Christ, you will cease from your own labor and you will begin to rest. I feel like I just got off of the boat in a new world and I don't know how to act. One thing I have learned from Noah is that you don't uncover people's nakedness in this new world. You do not expose their unrighteousness. We must walk backwards and cover them up because we are not to expose nakedness in this new world. We are not to point out their frailty, weakness or problems. We must bring them to the water to see the reflection of there new nature only then will they be loosed from there infirmity and be made straight.

I think another great way to explain this is by taking a look at Exodus 38:8 and the brazen laver in the Tabernacle of Moses. It was a basin made from the looking glasses of the women that assembled at the door of the tabernacle of the congregation. One day Moses decided to take a special offering. He told the women to bring their brass mirrors and give them as an offering. He then took those brass mirrors and beat them into a container that would hold water. That container would be filled with water from the smitten rock and we know later in the scripture that Jesus Christ is that smitten rock. He made this brass laver and filled it with water that would be used to wash the sacrifices and the hands and the feet of the priests. So when the priest would come up to this huge basin of water, he would wash his hands and his feet. He would wash also the sacrifices in this water that came from the smitten rock. Oh what a powerful picture of seeing ourselves through the redemptive work. First of all, the water came from the smitten rock and that rock was Christ. The laver being made from brass speaks of judgment. Always through the scriptures, brass speaks of judgment. So what we are seeing is ourselves through, not a judgment that is going to be, but through the judgment of the smiting of Christ. We are seeing ourselves through bloody water that has the blood of the sacrifice inside of it so that when we look at ourselves through the reflection of the blood. We can no longer see ourselves as undone and corrupt and full of sin. We must see ourselves as the express image of God and see His glory as we gaze into the face of this water.

Whatever the case, the fact remains that you cannot look into this mirror and behold your Genesis face or the face of your new birth and continue to act and perform differently than that which is your true identity. The only way you can be a hearer of the word and not a doer, is to forget that the man in the mirror is the new man.

I can't help but think that it is much like the movie The Lion King, where the prophet Rafiki comes and encounters a lion whose destiny it was to reign. He says to him, "My father left me; therefore, I am just out here in this desert, hanging out, eating slimy but satisfying things." But that prophet takes him to the water and when he looks into the water he sees his own reflection there. He tells the prophet, "My father told me he would never leave me, but he left me." Sad to say, but so many people have been told the same thing in churches around the world; that God leaves you every time you seem to make a mistake. The truth of it is, He will never leave you nor forsake you. He will not walk away from you. The prophet told the lion to look into the water and when he saw his own reflection he said, "That's just me." The prophet said, "Look within, my son, look deeper. Look within." I believe in this hour true prophetic ministries are coming on the scene to get you to look deeper, to look within. There you will discover that your Father doesn't just live on some planet three miles south of Mars, but He lives inside of you. When you see His reflection in you, you will rear back and roar like a lion. You will leave the desert, the wilderness, the diet of slimy but satisfying things. You will return to the rock; to the place you have been called to rule and reign as a king and a priest in the earth, such as this story of the woman who bowed to the earth. She is finding a new identity and it is empowering her not to stay in that condition. She is being loosed from this infirmity on the Sabbath day.

WOE, WOE, WOE OR HOLY, HOLY, HOLY?

This powerful picture can also be exemplified in Isaiah 5 and 6. I suggest that you read the whole text so that you can understand where I am coming from. Several times in the 5th chapter he begins to prophesy. He says woe to you who add house to house and lay field to field till no space is left for you to live alone in the land. Then he says to them woe unto them that draw iniquity with cords of vanity, and sin as it were with a cart rope. Woe unto them that call evil good, and good evil; that put darkness for light, and light for darkness; that put bitter for sweet, and sweet for bitter! Woe unto them that are wise in their own eyes, and prudent in their own sight! Woe unto them that are mighty to drink wine, and men of strength to mingle strong drink. He is prophesying several woes. He is a prophet in a real bad mood. He is prophesying woe, woe and woe. Have you ever been to one of those meetings where all you ever heard was the bad news? All you ever heard was how angry God was; how furious He was? You heard how much judgment was coming? And then all of a sudden God shows him a whole other dimension. In the 6th chapter he begins to see a totally different place. What really has happened is that he has been lifted up into the most holy place and he is seeing a view, not of the judgment seat, but of the mercy seat. He is seeing this time not what is going on in the earth, but he is seeing what is happening in the heavens.

When your focus is on what is happening in the earth, you will cry woe, woe, woe. You will preach how big the devil is, how bad the problems are, how the earth looks and how sinful man is. Once you get your head in the heavens, you will not cry woe, woe, woe. But Isaiah, in chapter 6, was lifted up into the mercy seat and began to hear the message that was being declared from this place as, "Holy, Holy, Holy is the Lord of Hosts; the whole earth is filled with His glory!"

It was such a shock to the system of Isaiah because, remember, he had just been preaching a woe, woe, woe revival. The book of Isaiah opens and he says, "In the year that King Uzziah died I saw also the Lord sitting upon a throne, high and lifted up and his train filled the temple." You see, when you get the focus away from the earthy and you begin to see that the Lord is upon the throne, high and lifted up, what you are going to see is the mercy seat.

Look at these parallels: Isaiah 6:2-5 KJV says, "Above it stood the seraphims: each one had six wings; with twain he covered his face, and with twain he covered his feet, and with twain he did fly. And one cried unto another, and said, Holy, Holy, Holy is the Lord of hosts: the whole earth is full of his glory. And the posts of the door moved at the voice of him that cried, and the house was filled with smoke. Then said I, Woe is me! for I am undone; because I am a man of unclean lips, and I dwell in the midst of a people of unclean lips: for mine eyes have seen the King, the Lord of hosts. Then flew one of the seraphims unto me, having a live coal in his hand, which he had taken with the tongs from off the altar: And he laid it upon my mouth, and said, Lo, this hath touched thy lips; and thine iniquity is taken away, and thy sin purged. Also I heard the voice of the Lord, saying, Whom shall I send, and who will go for us? Then said I, Here am I; send me."

The powerful picture that is being described here is when Isaiah began to see the most holy place. When you begin to see the throne room, which I believe is a picture of the mercy seat, he is not hearing the message of "woe, woe, woe", but heaven is declaring "holy, holy, holy." All of a sudden he declares, "My lips are unclean." The reason his lips were unclean was because he was not preaching heaven's message. He was preaching from the realm of the earthy and he was declaring something totally opposite than what heaven was saying. He was preaching woe, woe, woe and the seraphim are declaring holy, holy, holy. When he begins to realize that, he repents and says, "Take a coal from off that altar and touch my lips so that my message is no longer unclean." It is no longer a message of woe, woe, woe but a message of holy, holy, holy that will cause structural change to take place in the temple.

I think it is interesting to note that in the new covenant we are the temple of God and that our message is not one of woe, woe, woe focusing on who I am and what all I have done wrong, but my message is one of holy, holy, holy. I am focusing on what He has done, what He has accomplished and who He is so that it begins to cause the posts of the door to move. In other words, there will be some internal changes that take place. There will be some reconstruction and some things that occur inside of our temple as we begin to declare, "He is the King, and He is the Lord of hosts."

Much could be said here but I also want to just add this thought. There was a live coal that was taken in the hand of the seraphim and it was taken from the altar with the tongs. It is interesting to note that the altar of incense in the Tabernacle of Moses was lit by the fire that came from the sin offering in Leviticus 16:11-14. The point being made here is simply what was cleansing his lips was a message from the viewpoint of what the sin offering of Jesus Christ had really accomplished. It is an Old Testament picture of that which is to come in Christ.

If the fire that touches our lips is not from the viewpoint of the finished work of the sin offering, then it is strange fire and it is not acceptable unto God. Our lips must be touched with the fresh message of the finished Work of Jesus Christ and what His death, burial and resurrection as the sin offering has accomplished for us.

It is interesting to note that in the book of Revelation the prayer and praises of the saints are on this altar. What that simply tells me is that our prayer and our praise must be ignited. It must be empowered and must be influenced by a revelation of this sin offering. Once you truly know what Jesus did, it will cause you to pray differently. It will cause you to praise differently. It will cause you to preach differently. With your lips now cleansed you can say here am I send me. You will no longer preach woe, woe, woe, but declare holy, holy, holy; and then you will say to this woman called the church, "Woman, thou art loosed from this infirmity on this Sabbath day."

ENDNOTES

1. Don Kistler, *The Arithmetic of God* (God's Community Church of Charity, King's Mountain, NC. 1976) http://www.etpv.org/index.html

2. Reginald T. Naish, *Spiritual Arithmetic,* 3rd edition, (London: Seat. C.J. Thynne & Jarvis, Ltd. 28, White Friars Street, E.C. 4. 1926) Pg. 121.

3. Don Kistler, *The Arithmetic of God,* (God's Community Church of Charity, King's Mountain, NC. 1976) http://www.etpv.org/index.html

4. J. B. Jackson, *A Dictionary of Scripture Proper Names,* 3rd edition (Loizeaux Brothers, Neptune, NJ. 1957) Pg. 9.

Chapter Five

THE MAN WITH DROPSY

*"And it came to pass, as he went into the house of one of the chief Pharisees to eat bread on the Sabbath day, that they watched him. And, behold, there was a certain man before him which had the dropsy. And Jesus answering spake unto the **lawyers** and Pharisees, saying, Is it lawful to heal on the Sabbath day? And they held their peace. And he took him, and healed him, and let him go; And answered them, saying, Which of you shall have an ass or an ox fallen into a pit, and will not straightway pull him out on the sabbath day? And they could not answer him again to these things."* (Lk. 14:1-6 KJV.)

As I began to study the disease called dropsy I discovered the word "dropsy" is a term that was replaced by the word "edema". It was formally known as "dropsy". At www.wikipedia.org I found the definition of edema to be "a swelling due to the accumulation of excess fluid in any biological tissue. Edema has many root causes but the mechanism is simple; fluid is drawn from the blood into the tissues when there is a higher osmotic pressure in the tissues than in the blood. Many of the common conditions causing dropsy/edema are congestive heart failure, varicose veins, cirrhosis, allergic conditions, infection, bacterial toxins and kidney failure. Many times kidney failure can be caused by nutritional deficiencies; a lack of or low protein in the blood due to nutritional deficiency."

Perhaps what is pictured in this particular miracle is that Jesus is dealing with a change of diet. Perhaps He is dealing with nutritional deficiency. Especially edema was due to low serum protein in the blood. Low protein literally means a lack of meat. Perhaps what should be prescribed to this man would be a steady diet of more lamb.

Is it possible that many today in the church world are dying from heart problems? When I say that, I am not just talking about physical problems. I am talking about their hearts failing them for fear or, perhaps I am talking about hardening of the arteries. Hardened hearts can no longer sense the soft move of the Spirit of God tugging on their heartstrings because their hearts have become calloused by legalism and religious ritual.

Is it possible that their kidneys, which are purification organs, are failing? Maybe the kidneys spiritually are no longer filtering out the toxins and the disease and the bacteria that cause people to become discouraged and find them no longer able to walk in the things of God. Perhaps some of the injuries that have caused this edema in the saints of God could be the abuse and bruising and beatings we have taken that have caused us to become spiritually bruised and swollen. Once again, Jesus asks the lawyers and the Pharisees, "Is it lawful to heal on the Sabbath day?" In other places they would ask Him, "Why do you work on the Sabbath?" He said to them, "Because the Father works hitherto I work." You see, on the Sabbath day you cease from your labors and the Father and the Son go to work. When we rest, what happens is God does more in our rest than He ever does in our struggles and our labor. When I rest God works, and when I work God rests.

Perhaps honoring the Sabbath day to keep it holy is more than just taking a nap on Sunday. Perhaps it is simply saying, "I refuse to violate what Jesus already accomplished. I refuse to say that it is not enough and I am going to honor that by saying what Jesus finished work accomplished was certainly enough."

As I further researched this study, I found on the World Health Organization website a topic called epidemic dropsy. I discovered that in 1998 there were some states in India that were infected by epidemic dropsy. One of things I discovered was that the background for epidemic dropsy was that it was caused by the consumption of mustard oil that was adulterated with the oil of prickly poppy. This particular disease not only affected the heart, kidneys and liver, but it also affected the eyes. Some of the symptoms of epidemic dropsy are acute nausea, vomiting, loose motions, bloated stomach, arrhythmia and swelling of the hands and feet, known as edema. In extreme cases glaucoma and even death due to cardiac arrest have been reported. Also, one of the striking figures was that of kidney failure. Now you may say, "What does that have to do with anything?" The thing that really began to catch my attention was the fact that the mustard oil was contaminated with the oil of the prickly poppy. You say, "What does that mean?" Well let's take a closer look at it and see.

> *"Then said he, Unto what is the kingdom of God like? and whereunto shall I resemble it? It is like a grain of mustard seed, which a man took, and cast into his garden; and it grew, and waxed a great tree; and the fowls of the air lodged in the branches of it."* (Luke 13:18-19 KJV)

Then He uses the concept of the grain of mustard seed as being something that can define the kingdom of God. He begins to talk about when that seed is sown it becomes a great tree, which can lodge in its branches all the fowl of the air. What He is doing here is introducing a new form of governing.

For 1,500 years the law of the Mosaic system has been the form of rules that governed the people of God. But now Jesus is introducing a different form of government called the Kingdom of God. In the Kingdom of God it does not mean that you are lawless. It simply means that there is a new law that operates in your life, and that law is called the law of the Spirit of life that is in Christ Jesus. We begin to operate by faith and not by fear. We learn to be governed by the Spirit that dwells within.

Again, if you would take a look at Matthew 17:20, "And Jesus said unto them, Because of your unbelief: for verily I say unto you, If ye have faith as a grain of mustard seed, ye shall say unto this mountain, Remove hence to yonder place; and it shall remove; and nothing shall be impossible unto you." What He is doing in this text is showing them that faith is the currency of the new covenant. The only thing that is required in the new covenant is that you believe. Everything you do flows out of what you believe. When you see in Matthew 17 that He begins to use the concept of a mustard seed as a picture of faith and you understand that epidemic dropsy was caused by contaminated mustard seed, you might say, "What was the contaminant?" If you remember what I shared with you just a few lines above, it was contaminated with prickly poppy or thorny poppy. When I looked up the word Sinai where the Law of Moses was given, what I found is that the word Sinai simply means "my thorns". What this parable is speaking of and this miracle is, when you contaminate the mustard seed of faith and you contaminate kingdom government by mixing it with the law of Sinai with its thorns, you are causing people's hearts to begin to fail them. You are causing eyes to become blind. You are causing the purifying organs to no longer operate and function properly. You are causing varicose veins, edema and swelling that cause people to not be able to walk properly, and ultimately can produce spiritual death in them.

It is probably the spiritual epidemic of our day. It is used in the context where Jesus has just rebuked a devil and cast him out. The disciples ask Him, "Why could we not cast him out?" Jesus said, "Because of your unbelief." Is it possible that the more we preach the law, the more it shuts up faith? According to the book of Galatians, that is exactly what causes it.

> *"Knowing that a man is not justified by the works of the law, but by the faith of Jesus Christ, even we have believed in Jesus Christ, that we might be justified by the faith of Christ, and not by the works of the law: for by the works of the law shall no flesh be justified."* (Gal. 2:16 KJV)

"But before faith came, we were kept under the law, shut up unto the faith which should afterwards be revealed. Wherefore the law was our schoolmaster to bring us unto Christ, that we might be justified by faith. But after that faith is come, we are no longer under a schoolmaster. For ye are all the children of God by faith in Christ Jesus." (Gal. 3:23-26 KJV)

"But that no man is justified by the law in the sight of God, it is evident: for, the just shall live by faith. **And the law is not of faith**: *but, the man that doeth them shall live in them. Christ hath redeemed us from the curse of the law, being made a curse for us: for it is written, Cursed is every one that hangeth on a tree: That the blessing of Abraham might come on the Gentiles through Jesus Christ; that we might receive the promise of the Spirit through faith."* (Gal. 3:11-14 KJV)

It is very clear to me when I read these scriptures that one of the things that contaminated our faith has been the preaching of the law. We have preached from the thorny place of Mt. Sinai, and in so doing we have adulterated the mustard seed oil of faith that has caused spiritual dropsy. What we do mostly in the church is preach the parts of the law that fit our culture. Then we try to call that the Gospel when in reality it is what Paul called a perversion of the Gospel.

Is it any wonder that the longer most people sit in church, the less they believe and see the miraculous? Do you think that it could be caused by the fact that every time we get into the pulpit we tell the people why they don't receive is because there is sin in their life, whether a sin of commission or omission? The list goes on and on until the first thing that hits most people when they walk down a church aisle to try and receive a miracle from God is not necessarily faith but the thought that, "I believe God can do it, but will he do it for me?" Then all of the lists of why we are disqualified begin to flood our minds. Have we preached something that has deteriorated the faith and confidence of God's people? Have we contaminated this pure mustard seed of faith in the Kingdom of God by adding to it our ideas, concepts and traditions of men?

Perhaps it is time we preach the kingdom without mixture. Some will say, "We have to balance this or we have to balance that." What that usually means to them is that we have to mix just a little bit of law so that we can kind of control the people. But the truth is it is causing edema. It is causing heart problems, causing vision problems, causing us to begin to lose our ability to walk. Faith does not make you sit down and become a couch potato. Real faith causes you to get up and walk in what you believe to be true. I think the longer most people are in church, the more they learn what they don't believe.

People used to come and ask me, "What do you all believe up at that church?" I would start down the list of things that we do not believe. I would say, "Well, we don't believe that women should cut their hair. We don't believe that women should wear make-up. We don't believe that men should wear shorts. We don't believe that men ought to wear jewelry. We don't believe that you should watch TV. We don't believe that you should go to the theatre or the movie shows." We would go down the whole list of stuff that we do not believe in. And what I realized after a little while is that I had sat right in church and became an unbeliever. But the more I preach the grace of God and the Kingdom of God and the unforced rhythm of grace, the more my faith increases. I have become what I call a believer.

I always used to wonder when I traveled outside of the country, "Why does the miraculous seem to work in other places outside of America more so than it does in this country?" What I began to discover is that they have not been taught all of the unbelief and the rules and the regulations of man-made religion that deteriorates the faith of many and leaves them with nothing but the mixture of law and grace. The contaminated thorn from Mt. Sinai begins to shut up their faith and keep them from believing that they are qualified to receive the miracle. You see, if my miracle is based on me deserving it, I will walk away receiving nothing from the Lord. So many times we pray for someone on the basis of their credentials or we will start out by saying, "God, you should heal this person because they have been faithful to you. You should heal this person because they are in the ministry and they have served you and they have given up this or given up that." What we are doing is setting that person up for failure. If God is giving us something on the basis of how good we are instead of on the basis of how good He is, we are already disqualified to start. That is why it is called grace. It is the unmerited favor of God.

I think it is incredible that Jesus quotes many of these same words in Matthew 21:20-22. He begins to talk about faith again and talks about saying to this mountain, "Be removed and be cast into the sea." But the context of this verse is right behind Him cursing the fig tree. As I thought upon these concepts the first usage of the idea of the fig tree was clear back in Eden's garden when that was the tree that man used to cover his nakedness. He took the leaves of a fig tree to try and cover his nakedness. Perhaps what Jesus is cursing here is more than just some physical tree in the Middle East somewhere. Perhaps what He is cursing is the whole system of man's religion to try to cover his nakedness with his man-made self-help program. It is a man-made covering of a fig leaf. It is his works and his labor so that what he is really cursing here is his effort to try to make himself holy on the basis of that which he can put together, and what he can devise, and the apron that he can make. Jesus is cursing the whole idea of religion. It is only an apron and can only cover the front of you temporarily until it dries out and becomes crispy and falls off, which leaves you naked and ashamed. God's method of covering them in the garden was that He covered them with coats of skin. Something had to be sacrificed and blood had to be shed in order for them to be truly clothed. Does it not take us clear back to the idea of Adam in a garden where he simply says, "If I have enough information about good and evil I can now make myself like God." He made a declaration of independence and walked away from his dependency upon the Spirit of God to be the thing that would govern him. Then the only thing he was left with was a fig leaf or a fig tree covering. Jesus has now cursed that and says to them, "If you simply have faith you can not only say to this fig tree 'be cursed', but you also can say to this mountain, 'Be thou removed and be thou cast into the sea and it will be done.'" As I began to meditate on that, the Spirit of the Lord just began to breath to my heart and say to me, "This is not just walking out, taking any mountain; for example the Blue Ridge Mountains or the Allegheny Mountains, and trying to take that mountain and say to it 'be cast into the sea.'" Perhaps what he is dealing with is the removal of this mountain called Sinai. This connects to the fig tree that I talked about above, because Sinai is connected to that whole idea of works-based, man-made religion that tries to cover itself. Perhaps it is time to say to this mountain Sinai, "Be thou removed and be thou cast into the sea" and it will be done. Perhaps the sea that it is being cast into is not just found someplace in the Atlantic Ocean. But the sea He is talking about casting this mountain into is in Micah 7:18-19 where He talks about casting our sin into the sea of forgetfulness.

Let's compare a couple of scriptures with that thought in mind.

> *"And the second angel sounded, and as it were a great mountain **burning with fire** was cast into the sea: and the third part of the sea became blood; And the third part of the creatures which were in the sea, and had life, died; and the third part of the ships were destroyed."* (Rev. 8:8-9 KJV)

Now let's compare that scripture with this scripture.

> *"For ye are not come unto the mount that might be touched, and **that burned with fire,** nor unto blackness, and darkness, and tempest, And the sound of a trumpet, and the voice of words; which voice they that heard intreated that the word should not be spoken to them any more: (For they could not endure that which was commanded, And if so much as a beast touch the mountain, it shall be stoned, or thrust through with a dart: And so terrible was the sight, that Moses said, I exceedingly fear and quake:) But ye are come unto mount Sion, and unto the city of the living God, the heavenly Jerusalem, and to an innumerable company of angels."* (Heb. 12:18-22 KJV)

I don't think that it is an accident that the wording of these scriptures is almost so exact that it is incredible. Perhaps Revelation 8, "under the sound of the second trumpet" is dealing with the removing of this great mountain that burned with fire. It is connected to Mt Sinai in Hebrews 12, "for it is the mount that burned with fire". In this text it tells you that you did not come to that mountain; you did not come to blackness and darkness. You did not come to a voice that says, "Stay away." You did not come to fear and trembling. You did not come to the mountain that says you are going to be thrust through with a dart. You did not come to Mount Sinai. But in verse 22 it contrasts Mount Sinai with Mount Zion and says that you are, "Come to Mount Zion unto the city of the living God, the heavenly Jerusalem and to an innumerable company of angels." What He is showing you is the contrast between the old covenant Mount Sinai and the new covenant Mount Zion.

I submit to you, we are not marching to Zion, we are already in Zion. Mount Zion, according to this scripture, is the new covenant. In Hebrew 12:24 it says, "And to Jesus the mediator of the new covenant, and to the blood of sprinkling, that speaketh better things than that of Abel." We have come to a much better covenant. We have not come to a covenant that operates by fear. We have not come to the thorny contamination that contaminates the mustard seed of kingdom faith, but we have come to a mountain that says draw near with a true heart in full assurance of faith. Perhaps it is time for mountain moving faith. But the mountains that we need to move are not necessarily the Blue Ridge Mountains or the Allegheny Mountains or any other mountain range. Perhaps it is time to say to this mountain of legalism and law, "Be thou removed and be thou cast into sea." The sea we are casting it into is the sea of forgetfulness. Remember in the book of Revelation the sea became blood. Is it possible that when Jesus died and spilled His blood that He did not die for me but as me? His death was my death and that is why God remembers my sin no longer. Perhaps it is time to have the faith to be able to curse the fig tree system of self-help religious ideas that cannot cover man's nakedness, and begin to operate in mustard seed faith. That may be the smallest of all of the seeds that will ultimately become a great mountain that fills the whole earth.

> *"Then the angel that talked with me answered and said unto me, Knowest thou not what these be? And I said, No, my lord. Then he answered and spake unto me, saying, This is the word of the LORD unto Zerubbabel, saying, Not by might, nor by power, but by my spirit, saith the LORD of hosts. Who art thou, O great mountain? before Zerubbabel thou shalt become a plain: and he shall bring forth the headstone thereof with shoutings, crying, Grace, grace unto it."* (Zech. 4:5-7 KJV)

I am not suggesting that we have a lawless life, but that we learn how to live out of a different law called the law of the Spirit of life in Christ Jesus. This is where a different form of governing begins to govern our lives where the King of the kingdom has now taken up his abode within us. What causes our behavior to change is the inward working of the Holy Spirit that helps our infirmities and helps our weakness and also empowers us to be able to walk free from the contamination of legalism. It will remove all of the symptoms of epidemic dropsy. For the just shall live by faith are the words of the apostle Paul. When you truly believe that you are just and truly understand that your righteousness is not a product of your own human effort but the gift of God, the gift of righteousness and the abundance of grace empowers us to reign in life by one Christ Jesus. Then we understand that what governs us now is the Kingdom of God. That is what I believe Jesus was talking about in the very first chapter I wrote in this book that all of the law and the prophets spoke until John, and that violent men forced their way into it. Perhaps it is the hour when we must begin to no longer seize it by force and by human effort, labor and sweat. Is it not the season where we must simply begin to receive the Kingdom of God through the unforced rhythm of grace?

Consuming Fire

"And to Jesus the mediator of the new covenant, and to the blood of sprinkling, that speaketh better things than that of Abel. See that ye refuse not him that speaketh. For if they escaped not who refused him that spake on earth, much more shall not we escape, if we turn away from him that speaketh from heaven: Whose voice then shook the earth: but now he hath promised, saying, Yet once more I shake not the earth only, but also heaven. And this word, Yet once more, signifieth the removing of those things that are shaken, as of things that are made, that those things which cannot be shaken may remain. Wherefore we receiving a kingdom which cannot be moved, let us have grace, whereby we may serve God acceptably with reverence and godly fear: For our God is a consuming fire." (Heb. 12:24-29 KJV)

Later in Hebrews it tells us that we have, in fact, come to Jesus the mediator of a better covenant and that we should not refuse Him who speaks from this dimension. When he talks about refusing Him who spoke on earth, he is talking about the one who spoke from the old covenant, and now we must not turn away from Him who is speaking to us from heaven. What that simply says to me is that when we are speaking from heaven we are speaking from the viewpoint of the finished work. We are speaking from the viewpoint of how it is in Christ. We are speaking from a new covenant perspective. We are speaking a word that can not only shake the earth, but the heavens also. What he declares in this latter part of the book of Hebrews is that what causes the shaking is not because of terrorists, bombs or nuclear warfare. It is because there is a word being released from heaven that is shaking everything that can be shaken. One of the things that must be shaken, I believe in this hour, is that we must see that this whole religious system of legalism must be shaken by a word that flows from grace. When it does accomplish that, the result is we have received a kingdom which cannot be moved. Then it says very clearly,

"Let us have grace, whereby we may serve God acceptably with reverence and godly fear, for our God is a consuming fire." Perhaps this is not talking about future catastrophic events. It is talking about a sense of worship that I spoke of in other chapters; a sense of worship and awe and a sense of passion that is like a fire that burns in our hearts.

Not all fire has to be negative. When He baptized us in the Holy Ghost, He baptized with the Holy Ghost and with fire; then His fan is in His hand and will thoroughly purge His floor. It is the working of the Holy Spirit; our God who is a consuming fire that purges out of our lives the things He wants to remove. Perhaps He was also talking about the removing of the whole Mosaic system with its temple and animal sacrifices. Within a few short years after Paul the apostle wrote this book to the Hebrews, it would be literally burnt to the ground by the Romans in 70 A.D. Not one stone will be left on another in fulfillment of the prophecy of Jesus in Matthew 24. God would allow the Romans to so destroy the temple that it would be impossible to go back under the law even if they wanted. For without the temple and animal sacrifices the law could not truly be kept. Perhaps these are the things that were being shaken and removed and what was replacing it was the Kingdom of God with the inward governor called the Holy Spirit. Let's look at the scripture in light of this concept.

> *"For if we sin willfully after that we have received the knowl-edge of the truth, there remaineth no more sacrifice for sins, But a certain fearful looking for of judgment and fiery indignation, which shall devour the adversaries. He that despised Moses' law died without mercy under two or three witnesses: Of how much sorer punishment, suppose ye, shall he be thought worthy, who hath trodden under foot the Son of God, and hath counted the blood of the covenant, wherewith he was sanctified, an unholy thing, and hath done despite unto the Spirit of grace?"* (Heb. 10:26-29 KJV)

This Scripture has probably put more people in an insane asylum and tormented them with fear than any other Scripture when it is used incorrectly. As a matter of fact a psychiatrist told me that a high percentage of people that are in institutions either believe they have blasphemed the Holy Ghost or they have committed the unpardonable sin. Because they have been told that if they sin after becoming a believer, and they do it willfully, they are forever lost. If that is true then probably all of us are lost, because we have all sinned since we have been saved, and we did it willingly. If that be the case, we are better off not getting saved until right before we die so that our chances are greatly diminished of sinning willfully. What I discovered was that the word "sin" literally means to miss the mark. What the apostle Paul is talking about in this text is not doing some kind of sin-like anger. He is talking about missing the mark of this new covenant. He is talking about trampling underfoot the blood of the covenant. Because once you have been enlightened and received the knowledge of the truth concerning the blood of Jesus and the new covenant and then you go back under the law, you have to walk back over the blood of Jesus to get back to animal sacrifice. If you do, you are considering the blood of the covenant to be an unholy thing. You're trampling underfoot the Son of God and His precious blood. You are rejecting the Spirit of grace and you are saying what Jesus did is not enough. These Hebrews in about 67 A.D. were about to do just that. They were about to reject the new covenant with its extravagant grace. As a result, within three years or so a fiery judgment would come upon that nation that would consume it and dismantle its whole religious system. Because they chose the law over grace, God had to fulfill His promise to them and give them the curses of the law. Perhaps that is also what the apostle Peter meant when he said the elements were about to melt with fervent heat. Interestingly enough, the Greek word for elements is mostly used to describe the Law of Moses. Compare these scriptures. The word "elements" is the same Greek word and describes the Law of Moses.

> *"But the day of the Lord will come as a thief in the night; in the*
> *which the heavens shall pass away with a great noise, and the*
> ***elements*** *shall melt with fervent heat, the earth also and the*

*works that are therein shall be burned up. Seeing then that all these things shall be dissolved, what manner of persons ought ye to be in all holy conversation and godliness, Looking for and hasting unto the coming of the day of God, wherein the heavens being on fire shall be dissolved, and the **elements** shall melt with fervent heat?"* (2 Pet. 3:10-12 KJV)

Consider the possibility that the old heavens and the old earth was the passing away of the old covenant and the new heavens was the birthing of the new covenant. Since that form of governing was being dissolved what manner of life style would replace it? It would be one of holiness and godliness that is the result of a life full of grace and reverence the fruit of Christ living his life through us.

*"Even so we, when we were children, were in bondage under the **elements** of the world:"* (Gal. 4:3 KJV)

*"But now, after that ye have known God, or rather are known of God, how turn ye again to the weak and beggarly **elements**, whereunto ye desire again to be in bondage."* (Gal. 4:9 KJV)

Perhaps this is not talking about some future catastrophe, but simply the removing of the things that have been shaken, namely the old covenant. I don't know about you, but I want to fully embrace the blood of this covenant with its extravagant grace. In this new covenant there is no expectation of fiery judgment or indignation, only a confident expectation of good things.

I believe this shaking in Hebrews is very positive. It removes everything that is not the Kingdom of God so that what remains is simply the government of God in our lives. If we continue to mix the thorn of Sinai with the mustard seed of faith and of the kingdom, we will contaminate the faith and discourage people. What will happen is spiritual heart trouble and blindness. All of these things are symptoms of a wrong message. Once again the apostle

Paul calls the mixture of law and grace a perversion of the gospel in Galatians 1:17.

What we do is contaminate the message and then wonder why we get the results that we get. As I have said in previous chapters, when we preach the law we put people back up under the law. We put them back up under a curse. We must bless and curse not.

In my notes I began to do a study to compile a list of things that I call, "Things the Law Does." Here is some of that list:

1. Romans 4:15 "It works wrath".

2. Romans 5:20 "The law enters so that the offense would abound".

3. Romans 7:5 "The motions of sin are by the law and work in our members to bring forth fruit unto death".

4. Romans 7:8 "It wrought in me all manner of desire but without the law sin was dead". But it is what we preach over American pulpits every week.

5. Romans 7:9 "But I was alive without the law once but when the commandment came, sin revived and I died". So the preaching of the law revives sin and it revives death.

Is that not what the result of this contaminated mustard does — produce death? It brings a revival of sin, and it is what we preach out of our American pulpits every week. It is what created the roller coaster dilemma of the later part of Romans 7 where Paul would say, "When I want to do good, evil is present with me and what I hate, that's what I seem to do and what I desire to do of that which is good, I can't seem to perform." He is on the roller coaster ride of having the victory one day and being down the next. It is only when he discovers in Romans 8 that "there is therefore now no condemnation to them who are in Christ Jesus" that he begins to discover the freedom from this roller coaster. He begins to discover that the only way free from this roller coaster ride of ups and downs is to understand that only Christ can deliver us from the body of this death.

In I Corinthians 15:56 it says, "The strength of sin is the law and the sting of death is sin." Galatians 2:16 says, "By the works of the law no flesh will be justified." Galatians 3:10 says, "As many as are under the law, are under a curse." Perhaps the preaching of the law is what the book of Proverbs calls, "It is a way that seems right to a man and the end thereof is the ways of death." Notice it didn't say there is a way that is wrong. I believe it is one of the things that are defined as being in the flesh in the scriptures. For instance in Romans 7:5, "For when we were in the flesh, the motions of sin which were by the law did work at our members to bring forth fruit unto death." He defines in Romans 7:5 that when we were under the law, we were in the flesh. This helps me to clearly define one of the ways of looking at what it means to be in the flesh.

Perhaps it is not only talking about when you have a bad thought or you get angry, but perhaps one of the things that the scripture defines as being in the flesh; as when you are trying to do this by human effort and sweat. You are in the flesh and they that are in the flesh cannot please God. Galatians 3:2 says, "This only I want to learn of you: received ye the Spirit by the works of the law or by the hearing of faith? Are you so foolish? Having begun in the Spirit, are you now made perfect by the flesh?" He goes on to say in verse 5, "He therefore that ministers to you the Spirit and works miracles among you, did he do it by the works of the law or by the hearing of faith?" Once again, I believe that he begins to declare to us that one aspect of being in the flesh is simply that you are trying to do all of this through law and through human effort and sweat. As a matter of fact, I would just encourage you to read the entire book of Galatians. It is written to people who are trying to go back up under the law when Paul is trying to beseech them to move forward to the walk of the Spirit.

In Galatians 5 he beseeches them to stand fast in the liberty wherewith Christ has made them free and be not again entangled with the yoke of bond- age. He was not trying to get them to not go back to watching movies or to some other form of bondage. He is beseeching them not to go back under the law of the Mosaic system. As a matter of fact, he calls it leaven a little bit further in this chapter and says a little leaven leaveneth the whole lump. Perhaps this is the leaven of the scribes and Pharisees that Jesus said of which we must be aware. Perhaps it is the contamination of this prickly thorn that contaminates the faith. Because when we mix just a little bit of it, we contaminate the whole.

He later does declare unto us in Galatians 5:16 that if we walk in the Spirit we will not fulfill the lust of the flesh. Remember I told you in the list above that it is the law that stirs up in us the desire for sin. Therefore, it is the power of the Spirit to lift us above succumbing to the lust of the flesh. He goes on to describe to us the works of the flesh. They are listed in Galatians 5:19-21. What he is simply saying is that if you are under the law, this is what is going to be in your life; adultery, fornication, uncleanness, lasciviousness, idolatry, witchcraft, hatred, variance, emulations, wrath, strife, seditions, heresies, envyings, murders, drunkenness, revelings, and such. "Which I tell you before, as I have also told you in time past, that they which do such things shall not inherit the kingdom of God." He is not saying to them, "You can't go to heaven." He is saying these are enemies of living in the kingdom right now. The result of being in the Spirit, which to me, simply means you are no longer under the law, is that once you begin to operate out of the Spirit, fruit begins to result. Note that fruit is not something that we manufacture. It is love, joy, peace, longsuffering, joy, goodness, faithfulness, meekness, temperance; against such there is no law. In other words, if you are up under the law you are going to produce all of these bad things. But if you are in the Spirit you are producing the fruit of the Spirit. So many times we have preached the fruit of the Spirit as something you have to do by works, and we try to manufacture what we call fruit. What we do is create a beautiful basket of false, fake fruit, like you would see on someone's dinner table in the evening. Have you ever walked into someone's house and seen the most beautiful basket of fruit sitting on their table and say, "That peach looks good?" Then you reach down and grab that peach because it looks so good. You go to take a bite out of it and it is just plastic with peach fuzz. Can I tell you that is how the church is in this hour? It is simply plastic with peach fuzz and looks good on the table. It is a good ornament as a centerpiece, but there is no substance in it. I would rather have a peach with a bug bite in it that didn't look so good than I would to have plastic manufactured fruit. What we have done is put on fake fruit rather than reality of living out of the Spirit. The more we live out of the Spirit and the more that we walk in the Spirit, the more we are going to see these fruits manifest automatically and effortlessly. It will come from the unforced rhythm of grace.

Romans 6:14 says, "For sin shall not have dominion over you, for you are not under law but under grace." That says to me that it is not grace that causes people to sin. If you preach that greasy grace message you are just going to teach people to sin, but that is not what the scripture says. It says, "Sin will not have dominion over you because you are not under law but under grace." That just simply says that if you are under law, then sin will have dominion over you. But when you are under grace sin has lost its power. It is not grace that gives sin power. It is the law. Roman 10:4 says, "For Christ is the end of the law for righteousness to everyone that believeth."

HOLDING BACK HALF THE PRICE

One of the New Testament pictures of this is found in Acts 5:1-11. It is the story of Ananias and Sapphira. You may say, "Well how can these be examples of the mixture of law and grace?" It is very interesting that the word Ananias means grace and his wife's name was Sapphira. Sapphira is derived from a word that comes from when Moses was on the top of Mount Sinai and the body of heaven was open in all of its fullness. There God gave him the law. It was a pavement of blue Sapphire. This word Sapphire is derived from that exact same word in Exodus 24:10. What we have pictured here in the story of Ananias and Sapphira is the danger of mixing law and grace. Please note that it does not say that God killed these people. It says that they fell down dead upon hearing the words of Peter. You see, when we mix law and grace it is not

God that kills us, it is the mixture that kills us. It is causing spiritual dropsy! The biggest problem I have is not people who are simply ignorant of this truth. It is when we conspire to hold back half the price, and we don't preach the truth that Jesus paid the full price. He completely paid the debt of the law.

I believe there are many preachers today that know this truth and will not preach it for fear that they will lose control of the people. However, I say to them, "You've never controlled them to start with." When we conspire to hold back half the price, and we do not preach that Jesus paid it all, we are causing spiritual death to occur and dropsy that is in epidemic proportions. We must not mix law and grace. I think it is incredible that just a few chapters later, Saul of Tarsus was knocked to the ground and was blinded for 3 days and 3 nights. The 3 days and 3 nights powerfully picture the 3 days and 3 nights of the person and work of Jesus Christ. That is what this man Saul, who was a Pharisee of the Pharisees and under the Law of Moses at this point was blind to. I think it is incredible to note that there was a man by the name of Ananias, in other words "grace without law". He comes and touches the eyes of this Saul of Tarsus and he becomes Paul the Apostle, who becomes the greatest apostle of grace that ever walked. Oh that God would just deliver us from the mixture of law and grace and from the contamination of this kingdom faith mustard seed with the prickly, thorny concepts of Sinai!

We must not mix law and grace. We must not mix Ananias and Sapphira. We especially cannot conspire to hold back half of the price. We must preach that Jesus paid it all. You see, the fulfilling of the law does not denote that Jesus just did away with something and put it to the side. The Bible says that He did not come to destroy the law but He came to fulfill it in Matthew 5.

It would be to me as if I owed someone a covenant of $10,000 for an automobile and I enter into a covenant to pay that $10,000 over a 10 month period. Once I pay the 10th month of $1,000 then I did not do away with that covenant. I have fulfilled it. That is what Jesus did in His redemptive work. He did not come to do away with the law. He so completely met every requirement that it had. He so totally fulfilled every sin offering, every wave offering, every sheath offering, and every demand that a righteous God could make for the law. Jesus paid it in full and rolled it together as a great scroll and said this covenant has been completely paid in full. He did not do away with it. He paid it off. Now that's something to shout about!

What is tragic to me is that here we are 2000 years into the new covenant, still trying to make payments on a covenant that Jesus completely and totally fulfilled. I refuse to hold back half the price. I refuse to mix law and grace. I refuse to contaminate faith with my ideas of religion and perversion of the gospel. I profess to know nothing among you but Christ and Him crucified.

THE TREATMENT FOR DROPSY

In my research on the World Health Organization website I discovered that the only management of this epidemic dropsy was to have a diet that was rich in protein. Immediately when I saw that, I thought that we just need to eat more lamb because the more we feed on the lamb and His finished work, the more it delivers us from this mixture. In Exodus 12 it was feeding on the lamb that delivered the children of Israel from bondage. He told them that they were not to water down the lamb. If we preach watered down lamb we will get watered down results. He told them to eat not of it raw. In other words, if it isn't done, don't eat it. Or if it's not finished work, don't put it in your mouth.

In my research I also found that all age groups were affected, but there was one exception to this epidemic. The only ones who were immune from this epidemic dropsy were breast fed infants. As soon as I saw that the Spirit of God just went off in my heart and said that, "Those that are exempt from this disease are those that are fed on the sincere milk of the Word." We need to understand that the idea of milk is connected to righteousness.

> *"For when for the time ye ought to be teachers, ye have need that one teach you again which be the first principles of the oracles of God; and are become such as have need of **milk**, and not*

*of strong **meat**. For every one that useth milk is unskilful in the word of righteousness: for he is a babe."* (Heb. 5:12-13 KJV)

It says that everyone that uses milk is unskillful in the word of righteousness, for he is a babe. Can you image what would happen if we taught a newborn Christian from the first day as a believer as he enters the church, to be fed on a steady diet of righteousness by faith instead of the Law of Moses and rejection? It is a righteousness that is not a product of the law, but by faith. I want you to also remember that milk was one of the elements of the Promised Land. It is one of the results of being in this Promised Land called Christ; in this Promised Land called rest. When we enter into the finished work of Christ, we enter into a land that flows with milk and honey. It is the word of righteousness that proceeds from this land to people. It will make everything right that will cause strong bones to be built in our spiritual bodies and deliver us from this epidemic dropsy.

In Romans 1:16-17 the Gospel of Christ is what reveals the righteousness of God from faith to faith, and it continues to declare that the just shall live by faith. In other words, when we feed on this word about Christ and His finished work and we continue to feed on the sincere milk of the Word, it produces a faith in us that will cause us to live by what we believe to be true. If we believe that we are righteous, we are going to act like we are righteous.

Romans 3:21 tells us, "But now the righteousness of God without the law is manifested, being witnessed by the law and the prophets." If you read the entire book of Romans what you will find is that from chapter 1 through the last part of Chapter 3 is that the whole purpose of the law was to conclude all under sin so that He could have mercy on all. In these same chapters He is disqualifying just about everybody and everything. The whole purpose is so that He might conclude all under sin so He can have mercy on all. He wants to show us that there are only two ways in the scripture whereby you can be made righteous. The first one was by keeping all of the rules and regulations of the old covenant, and the second one was simply by believing in the One who did. Then He begins to unfold from Romans 4 and on, how Abraham's faith was counted to him for righteousness even before the law came, and even before he was circumcised, even before he produced a son or did anything. He simply believed God and it was counted to him for righteousness. He believed God's promise that He was able to perform what He promised. Then he said, "Amen" to God. God counted that to him as righteousness.

Oh dear one, can you believe God today when He promises to you what He started in you that He will finish and perform? Can you say "amen" to Him and trust the power of the Holy Spirit to work in you? If you can do that and believe that God can finish the work, then He accounts it to us for righteousness.

He clearly tells them in Romans 4:13, "For the promise, that he should be the heir of the world, was not to Abraham, or to his seed, through the law, but through the righteousness of faith." Then again he confirms that in Romans 5:17 by telling us that because of the abundance of grace and the gift of righteousness, we reign in life by one Jesus Christ. He calls righteousness in Romans 5:17 a gift. What part of gift don't we understand? A gift means you didn't pay for it. Somebody else has paid for it and given it to you as a free gift.

He tells us in Romans 9:30-31 that the Gentiles did not follow after righteousness, but they have attained righteousness. They have attained to righteousness, even the righteousness which is of faith. But Israel, which followed after the law of righteousness, hath not attained to the law of righteousness. In verse 32 they sought it not by faith, but as it were, by the works of the law and they stumbled at the stumbling block. In Romans 10:3 it says, "For they being ignorant of God's righteousness, and going about to establish their own righteousness, have not submitted themselves unto the righteousness of God." Romans10:4 says, "For Christ is the end of the law for righteousness to everyone who believes." He tells us in I Corinthians 15:34 that if we will awake to righteousness then we will sin not. II Corinthians 5:21 tells us how we became righteous. It says, "For he hath made him to be sin for us who knew no sin that we might be made the righteousness of God in him." In other words, He who did absolutely nothing wrong, who was the sinless, spotless Lamb of God, was made to be sin. That doesn't seem fair to me, but it also doesn't seem fair that I, who did absolutely nothing right, could be made righteous. What an incredible exchange. He was made sin. I was made righteous. In other words, He took what I had coming so I could get what He has coming. He took my sin so that I could have His righteousness. Galatians 2:21 says, "I do not frustrate the grace of God: for if righteousness comes by the law, then Christ is dead in vain."

You see, in the new covenant, righteousness is not a result of your performance. It is a gift. Again, what part of gift don't we understand? Here is one other thought on righteousness.

> *"And when he is come, he will reprove the world of sin, and of righteousness, and of judgment: Of sin, because they believe not on me; Of righteousness, because I go to my Father, and ye see me no more; Of judgment, because the prince of this world is judged."* (John 16:8-11 KJV)

These scriptures describe three dimensions of the work of the Holy Spirit in the life of the believer. The first work of the Holy Spirit is to convict and convince the world of sin because they believe not. When you are not a believer then the power of the Holy Spirit must come upon you to convince and convict of sin because all have sinned and come short of the glory of God. Once you have repented and become a believer, then the second dimension of the work of the Holy Spirit is that it must convince you of righteousness. I am praying that God would release the same power of conviction in the life of the believer as He did when I was not saved. That could convict me of my sin and let me realize that I needed a Savior. If the Holy Spirit had the power that it did to convict and convince me of sin and draw me to an altar of prayer where I could accept the Lord Jesus Christ into my life, then the Holy Spirit has that same power to convict and convince me of righteousness. When I become convicted of righteousness what I find is that I no longer want to do the former things. Following that is the third dimension of the work of the Holy Spirit that is to convince the world of judgment because the prince of this world has already been judged. He convicts me first of all of sin because

I need to come to Him by faith. Secondly he convicts me of righteousness. Thirdly, as a believer, I am convinced that my judgment is not in my future. My judgment is in my past, and as a believer my judgment was fully met at the cross of Jesus Christ.

I think it is incredible that the apostle Paul in Philippians 3 begins to give his testimony of what he was delivered from. In one place Paul would say something like, "I'm the chief of sinners." In other words, I would think if Paul was the chief of sinners he must have been into sex, drugs and rock and roll, or what many of us would call sin. Then he begins to give as his testimony that he was delivered from performance-based religion. He says that we are the circumcision which worshipped God in the Spirit and have no confidence in the flesh. When he said that we don't have any confidence in the flesh, it did not mean that he could not trust Peter or trust James. What he is saying is, "I don't have any confidence in my own ability to produce this. I don't have any confidence in my flesh to produce this righteousness." Remember what I wrote just a few pages before, that being in the flesh means you are trying to do this by human effort and through the works of the law. You are tilling the ground of human sweat and effort and all you get is more cursed thorns. Jesus wore a crown of thorns to redeem you from this contaminated thinking. He goes on to say in verse 4 of Phil. that though I might have confidence in the flesh, if any other man thinks that he hath whereof he might trust, he said I more. He is giving his religious credentials because that is what caused him to miss the mark of the new covenant. Then he begins to give his testimony. "As I was circumcised the eighth day, of the stock of Israel, of the tribe of Benjamin, an Hebrew of the Hebrews; as touching the law, I was a Pharisee; Concerning zeal, persecuting the church; touching the righteousness which is in the law, blameless. But what things were gain to me, those I counted loss for Christ. Yea doubtless, and I count all things but loss for the excellency of the knowledge of Christ Jesus my Lord: for whom I have suffered the loss of all things, and do count them but dung, that I may win Christ."

Isn't that incredible that what Paul says he was delivered from was religion? He was delivered from a performance-based religion that was nothing more than the contamination of the thorny, prickly poppy of Sinai that was contaminating New Testament righteousness. He said that, "I had to count that as dung." In verses 9-10 he said, "He would be found in him, not having mine own righteousness, which is of the law, but that which is through the faith of Christ, the righteousness which is of God by faith: That I may know him, and the power of his resurrection, and the fellowship of his sufferings." What Paul began to discover is that this righteousness is not a product of performance. He had been delivered from this epidemic dropsy. Perhaps that is what caused Paul's blindness. Remember eye problems was one of the symptoms of dropsy Perhaps that is what is being pictured in the story of the man with Dropsy.

In my studies I found that the only preventive measure to keep people from getting epidemic dropsy was to prevent and refrain from using the mustard oil that was contaminated with the thorns.

Oh dear ones, I believe that when we begin to feed people on the sincere milk of the Word, they will become immune to this disease! When we feed them on a steady diet of righteousness by faith, we feed them on a diet of grace without the works of the law. Faith will begin to arise in the hearts of people afresh and new. They will not find themselves crippled and unable to walk, but their eyes that had been blinded by this dropsy will be flooded with the light of the glorious gospel of grace. Their hearts that have failed them for fear, their organs that have not functioned properly to purify them will be made whole by the power of God on this Sabbath day. The miraculous will break forth in every dimension. Seek ye first the kingdom of God and HIS righteousness and all these things will be added to you. It is a perpetual rest and as we feed on the finished work of Christ, we will awake to righteousness and sin no more.

Chapter Six

THE POOL OF BETHESDA

"After this there was a feast of the Jews; and Jesus went up to Jerusalem. Now there is at Jerusalem by the sheep market a pool, which is called in the Hebrew tongue Bethesda, having five porches. In these lay a great multitude of impotent folk, of blind, halt, withered, waiting for the moving of the water. For an angel went down at a certain season into the pool, and troubled the water: whosoever then first after the troubling of the water stepped in was made whole of whatsoever disease he had. And a certain man was there, which had an infirmity thirty and eight years. When Jesus saw him lie, and knew that he had been now a long time in that case, he saith unto him, Wilt thou be made whole? The impotent man answered him, Sir, I have no man, when the water is troubled, to put me into the pool: but while I am coming, another steppeth down before me. Jesus saith unto him, Rise, take up thy bed, and walk. And immediately the man was made whole, and took up his bed, and walked: and on the same day was the sabbath. The Jews therefore said unto him that was cured, It is the sabbath day: it is not lawful for thee to carry thy bed. He answered them, He that made me whole, the same said unto me, Take up thy bed, and walk. Then asked they him, What man is that which said

unto thee, Take up thy bed, and walk? And he that was healed wist not who it was: for Jesus had conveyed himself away, a multitude being in that place. Afterward Jesus findeth him in the temple, and said unto him, Behold, thou art made whole: sin no more, lest a worse thing come unto thee. The man departed, and told the Jews that it was Jesus, which had made him whole. And therefore did the Jews persecute Jesus, and sought to slay him, because he had done these things on the Sabbath day. But Jesus answered them, My Father worketh hitherto, and I work. Therefore the Jews sought the more to kill him, because he not only had broken the sabbath, but said also that God was his Father, making himself equal with God." (John 5:1-18 KJV)

Several things in this text get my attention very quickly. The first one is that Jesus is attending a feast of the Jews. According to Adam Clark's commentary, this feast is probably the feast of Passover for several reasons. Number one, they were at a sheep market and it was the place that sheep were led to slaughter on the feast of Passover. This sheep market was also called the sheep gate. A careful study of the book of Nehemiah will reveal there was a gate called the sheep gate.

As I have studied the maps of ancient Jerusalem and looked at many of the comments concerning this pool, I discovered that the sheep would be brought in through the sheep gate to this location. Then they would be taken to the sheep market where the sacrifice would then be washed and sacrificed. Many times the blood from the sacrifice would spill into the water and run down the slope into this pool called Bethesda. Legend has it that the blood is probably what troubled the water. When the blood of the sacrifice would come into that pool it would cause healing effects to flow from the sacrifice.

Secondly, in the Hebrew tongue it is called Bethesda, which literally means "the house of mercy." Thirdly, it had five porches. In these lay a great multitude of impotent folk who were blind, halt, withered, all waiting for the moving of the water.

There is a considerable amount of powerful symbolism here that catches my attention. Simply it is because everything is setting us up to see the power of the redemptive work of the true Lamb of God, Jesus Christ. When He comes on the scene He says to a man who was waiting to be healed and waiting on a certain season for the water to be troubled, "Do you want to be made whole?" Please note that He does not say, "Do you simply want to be healed?" He says, "Do you want to be made whole?" I think the idea here is that Jesus is going to do more than just heal his physical body. He wants to make him whole - spirit, soul and body. He has come to the ultimate sheep gate, Jesus Christ, who is the door into the sheepfold. The true Shepherd, the true lamb, the true Sacrifice is now standing there. This man under an old covenant was sitting there waiting on a certain season or a certain time. He was waiting on the Passover feast so that the blood from the sacrifice might perhaps trouble the water and he could be the first one in. But now the ultimate of Passover is standing in front of him. The ultimate Lamb of God, the ultimate Sabbath day is standing in front of him, literally, at a pool called Bethesda which means "the house of mercy." God's mercy wrapped up in human flesh is now standing before him. It is not an accident that this place had five porches. The number five is the number of grace.

Isn't it amazing that in an old covenant concept of God many people lay at the very gate of the power of God and the redemptive work of Jesus Christ. They are still impotent, blind, halt and withered. They want some season to come or a certain messenger or angel or preacher to come to town to trouble the water so that they might possibly be healed. I think what Jesus is doing here is shifting our thinking from an old covenant mentality to a new covenant mentality concerning these things. In the new covenant there are not just certain seasons and certain times. The time is always now in God's agenda in the new covenant because the Lamb of God is the true House of Mercy. The true grace of God and the true water that flows from the sacrifice of the true Lamb of God is available to us at any given time that we can find ourselves accessing it.

Last, but not least, there was a certain man there that had an infirmity for 38 years. As I began to do a careful study of that, I found that Deuteronomy 2:14 tells us that was the exact length of time that the children of Israel were in the wilderness journey until the men of war died; until they had crossed over getting ready to go into the Promised Land. They had wandered for 38 years.[1]

In Hebrews 4 the Promised Land is more than a piece of real estate. It is the rest of God that is enjoyed because of the finished work of Christ.

One of the things that I began to say early on in this book is in Matthew 11 where we started. We told you that all the law and prophets spoke until John, and that violent men forced their way into the kingdom. But now in the New Testament we do not have to force our way or violently seize the kingdom, we simply have to receive it. We simply have to learn how to flow in the unforced rhythms of grace. That's why it is called the gospel of peace. I think it is also interesting to note that Isaiah 40:1-3 KJV says, "Comfort ye, comfort ye my people, saith your God. Speak ye comfortably to Jerusalem, and cry unto her, that her warfare is accomplished, that her iniquity is pardoned: for she hath received of the Lord's hand double for all her sins. The voice of him that crieth in the wilderness, Prepare ye the way of the Lord, make straight in the desert a highway for our God." Isn't it interesting those are the very words that were used to describe John the Baptist? Whenever John came on the scene, he was the voice of one crying in the wilderness. John was about to introduce the true Lamb of God. Did he not say when Jesus was walking down over the muddy banks of the Jordan River, "Behold the Lamb of God who takes away the sin of the world?" That is why I can comfort God's people and say to them their iniquity is pardoned. In the person and work of Jesus Christ we have received double for all our sins. Jesus paid it all. I can declare a gospel of peace because the battle was won over 2000 years ago and our warfare is accomplished. We can now beat our swords and weapons into plowshares and our spears into pruning hooks and not learn war anymore.

There is a house of mercy that is available to us right now. There is a cleansing flow of blood and water that flows from Christ that has the power to make the most withered, impotent, weak, blind person completely whole - spirit, soul and body. The message must shift from an old covenant mentality that is always waiting on an angel to come down and trouble the water. You don't have to wait any longer because wrapped up in the person of Jesus Christ is the house of mercy and flowing from this Lamb of God is blood and water that can cure the infirmity of the human family.

Something that could also be mentioned at this point is that this was a sheep market. It is the place where they bought and sold sheep. Isn't it a sad tragedy today that in many cases the American church has literally become a sheep market? It is the place where we trade sheep and what we call church growth in America is simply sheep changing stalls. We are buying, selling and trying to make merchandise of God's sheep and God's people by pointing them to one individual messenger, one angel or one preacher that has the power to stir the waters. Many never teach them that the same Spirit that raised Christ from the dead dwells inside of them and that in the new covenant they have the same power inside of them as any other ministry or preacher. Oh, I think this is a day of not just making great preachers, but making great people. It is time to equip the Saints to do the work of service.

I heard a great missionary say one time that when he had been in Russia the people came to him and said, "When the preachers from America come here and they leave, we know that they are great, but when you come here and leave, we know that we are great." Oh that God would challenge our hearts not to just make names for ourselves, not to just be trading sheep, but to make the people of God know that they are great. We need to teach them that the same Spirit that raised Christ from the dead dwells in them. I believe that we will release such a powerful ministry from the body of Christ to the world, knowing that they are not just waiting on some messenger to trouble the waters or some angel to come down. Nor are they waiting for a certain season. Several times in Hebrews 3 and 4 the Holy Spirit continues to say today, after so long a time today, while it is called today, etc. You see, a procrastinator is somebody who will not take now for an answer. We are always saying some glad morning and God is always living in the present. I believe the generation is now on the scene that is mixing the word with faith. They are rising to say this is the day, now is the time, let us lay hold of it. And milk and honey which symbolizes incredible provision and the miraculous begins to flow from this Promised Land called rest.

Jesus is Greater than Angels

"God, who at sundry times and in divers manners spake in time past unto the fathers by the prophets, Hath in these last days spoken unto us by his Son, whom he hath appointed heir of all things, by whom also he made the worlds; Who being the brightness of his glory, and the express image of his person, and upholding all things by the word of his power, when he had by himself purged our sins, sat down on the right hand of the Majesty on high: Being made so much better than the angels, as he hath by inheritance obtained a more excellent name than they." (Heb. 1:1-4 KJV)

In this text it tells us that in times past God spoke to the fathers by the prophets. But in these last days, He has spoken to us by His Son whom He has made heir of the worlds. Let me first say that I believe Paul the apostle wrote this book to the Hebrews. The word Hebrews comes from a root word that literally means "to cross over" or "the crossers over". What is happening in this text is that they are crossing over, but this time they are not crossing over a physical Jordan River. They are crossing over out of an old covenant into the new covenant. When the apostle Paul said in verse 2 that, "God hath in these last days spoken unto us by His Son", he was not talking about the last days of this age. He was talking about the last days of the age of the law or the Mosaic system, which had now come to an end.

Remember that this man laid at the pool for 38 years and again 38 was the length of time they were in the wilderness journey, until the men of war had died. Perhaps we have come to another crossing over. Perhaps God is speaking to us about crossing over; moving away from waiting on men and angels troubling the water. In the new covenant He has brought us to the Son with access to a greater One than the angels. Jesus was made so much better than the angels and has by inheritance obtained a more excellent name. Remember, this man was waiting on an angel to come down and trouble the water. But something greater is being introduced here in this powerful picture of the redemptive work of Christ. There is somebody better than an angel that is now on the scene who has come to be the mediator of a better covenant. This water is flowing from the true Lamb of God. It is not a seasonal stirring. It is water that will continue to be troubled so that anybody who accesses this true flow out of this redemptive work will not only be made whole physically, but they will be made whole - spirit, soul and body. I would encourage you to read the whole of Hebrews 1 and 2. Again, the book of Hebrews is full of more excellent things. But in the first two chapters he simply begins to show that Jesus is much better than angels. Hebrews 1:13-14 says, "But to which of the angels said he at any time, Sit on my right hand, until I make thine enemies thy footstool? Are they not all ministering spirits, sent forth to minister for them who shall be the heirs of salvation?" Hebrews 2:5 says, "For unto the angels hath he not put in subjection the world to come, whereof we speak?" Hebrews 2:9 says, "But we see Jesus, who was made a little lower than the angels and for the suffering of death, crowned with glory and honour; that he by the grace of God should taste death for every man." Verses 14-18 of chapter 2 says, "Forasmuch then as the children are partakers of flesh and blood, he also himself likewise took part of the same; that through death he might destroy him that had the power of death, that is, the devil; And deliver them who through fear of death were all their lifetime subject to bondage. For verily he took not on him the nature of angels; but he took on him the seed of Abraham. Wherefore in all things it behooved him to be made like unto his brethren, that he might be a merciful and faithful high priest in things pertaining to God, to make reconciliation for the sins of the people. For in that he himself hath suffered being tempted, he is able to succor them that are tempted."

Oh, can you just see the powerful pool of Bethesda that is standing there in the person of Jesus Christ? He is the One who has come to deliver us! It is His sacrificial blood flowing into the stream of the Spirit that releases the flow of mercy. He is the house of mercy personified. It is because of His redemptive work that the miraculous is being released in this environment. That is what is being pictured here. Greater than Angels is now on the scene. He is a merciful high priest. He has brought us to the house of Bethesda, the house of mercy. He has come to release grace which again is symbolized by the five pillars that are there. Notice he tells this man to go and sin no more. He empowers him to do exactly that when He says to him, "Take up your bed and walk." He does not just give him a commandment when He says to him, "Go and sin no more." He gives him the grace, or empowerment not to sin. For those of us who may be crippled in some area of our lives, we can come to Him and find grace to help our infirmities, whether spiritual or physical. Thank God He does not just simply give us a commandment. He gives us grace that supernaturally empowers us. He does not give us a law. He gives us His life. He is now living inside of us and He is able to succor them that are tempted, because He was tempted in all manner, like as we. It is high time that we recognize that every one of us is crippled in some way or another. We cannot walk this out apart from His indwelling life empowering us. Without Him we can do absolutely nothing. With Him we can do all things through Christ who strengthens us. You see, He gives more grace to the humble. Humility does not mean that we go around with our heads hung down saying I'm worthless. It means I humble myself and say I cannot do this on my own. I need His help. I am powerless over my weaknesses. It is when I humble myself under the mighty hand of God that He raises me up and empowers me to go and sin no more.

You want to talk about wholeness! This is more than just a temporary fix. This is more than someone just getting their legs, eyes or withered bodies touched. This is Jesus trying to show them that something better is going to transpire from this posture of rest, and from this perpetual Sabbath day. He tells that man very simply, "Rise, take up your bed and walk." The bed here symbolizes rest.

This brings much controversy as the religious leaders of His day were not so much concerned because He had healed the man, but because He told him to take up his bed and walk. What that pictures to me is the fact that the posture of rest does not make a spiritual couch potato out of you. What it simply does is make you understand that everything that you are now receiving, everything that you are now enjoying, is now coming from the posture of rest. This is a result of the finished work of Christ. I believe that is what is symbolized in this man carrying his bed. When they asked Jesus why He had done these things on the Sabbath day His response was, "My Father worketh hitherto and I work." On the Sabbath day you cease from your labors and the Father and the Son go to work. But it doesn't make you a spiritual couch potato. It simply means you are walking out of the finished work of the cross of Jesus Christ. You see, if you work, God will rest and when you rest God will work. It is God who works in me both to will and to do His own good pleasure.

Oh dear one, you will not be able to continue to sin once you are truly gripped by the message of grace. Once you see the finished work and what all Jesus has done for you, and who He is inside of you, you will rise and take up your bed and begin to walk from the posture of rest, knowing that you have been made whole. A man that is whole cannot help but to walk in righteousness. You will no longer work to get salvation but you will work out of the salvation you already have.

Hallelujah! You certainly have come to the true House of Mercy to the ultimate Sheep Gate. You have certainly come to the five porches of His grace. You have come to that which pictures all of the person and work of the atoning work of Jesus Christ. You have come to the ultimate Passover and the ultimate Sabbath day. I would say to you, "Rise, take up your bed and walk. Go and sin no more."

Endnote

1. *The Companion Bible,* under Bullinger's notes (Zondervan Bible publishers, Grand Rapids, MI. 1974) Pg. 240.

Chapter Seven

THE MAN BORN BLIND

"And as Jesus passed by, he saw a man which was blind from his birth. And his disciples asked him, saying, Master, who did sin, this man, or his parents, that he was born blind? Jesus answered, Neither hath this man sinned, nor his parents: but that the works of God should be made manifest in him. I must work the works of him that sent me, while it is day: the night cometh, when no man can work. As long as I am in the world, I am the light of the world. When he had thus spoken, he spat on the ground, and made clay of the spittle, and he anointed the eyes of the blind man with the clay, And said unto him, Go, wash in the pool of Siloam. He went his way therefore, and washed, and came seeing." (John 9: 1-7 KJV)

This powerful story so pictures the whole human family who was born blind from our birth. Sometimes we are blind not only in our physical birth, but even our new birth. Many of us sit in religious systems where we are blinded to the person and work of Jesus Christ.

His disciples asked Him who sinned. When you have an old covenant mentality and you are not seeing things from the posture of the Sabbath day, you are on a sin hunt. You are always looking for someone to blame for your problem. They asked Him, "Who did sin, this man or his parents?" that he was born blind. Now I don't know about you but I think that is a fairly absurd question "Did this man sin?" How in the world could he have sinned if he was born blind? On the way out of the birth canal did he somehow sin? If that is not enough to blame, then we have to look for blame in his parents. I guess if you are looking at things from an old covenant viewpoint, you might look back and say, "Well the sins of the father's are being visited to the 3rd and 4th generations." In previous chapters I have already taught you some things that show you how on the cross Jesus took the cup of the sour grapes that set the teeth of the children on edge. He took all of our generational curses to the cross with Him. Therefore, the condition of this man was not on the basis of his sin or his parents. It is sad to say that even still in this day, 2000 years into the new covenant, we have such sin-conscious preaching in the American church. It is bad enough that folk are preaching the law and what is sin under the law. Then we come up with all of the manmade rules and traditions; ideas and concepts of men that are mostly cultural. Many of these concepts only preach in a certain culture. I believe Jesus was not on a sin hunt in this particular case. I already told you in previous chapters that the second dimension of the work of the Holy Spirit is not to continually convince you of sin. That is only the work of the Holy Spirit when you are not a believer. Once you become a believer the work of the Holy Spirit is to convince and convict you of righteousness and that you are in fact righteous on the basis of the gift of righteousness.

As a matter of fact, if you would go back and even study the sin offering of the Old Testament when the sinner would come to God, he would have to come through the mediator of a priest and he would have to bring a spotless lamb or sacrifice for a sin offering. He would then lay his hands on that lamb, give it to the priest and the priest would confess the sins over that lamb. He would then take that lamb and examine the lamb from head to toe to see whether or not the lamb was spotless. If the lamb was spotless it would be accepted as a sin offering. The thing that I want you to notice is that the sinner was never examined, only the lamb. The basis of our acceptance in the new covenant is not on the basis of how good I am or on the basis of whether I sinned or did not sin. My acceptance in the new covenant is on the basis of how perfect my Lamb is and whether or not my priest accepts that Lamb. Of course, we know that when John the Baptist was standing on the bank of the Jordan River he pointed Jesus out and said, "Right there is the Lamb of God who takes away the sin of the world." That Lamb was later examined by Pilate and examined by the high priest. Pilate would then wash his hands and say, "I am innocent of the blood of this man because this is innocent blood." Even Judas would have to testify concerning this as he went back to the temple. Remember, in the scriptures Jesus called Judas a devil. It is interesting to me that even the devil has to testify in the case of Jesus. What he said when he went back into the temple is, "I have betrayed innocent blood." Even the devil had to testify that the Lamb Christ Jesus was spotless. Therefore, you and I are accepted today not on the basis of what we have done, but on the basis of what this sacrifice has done. Because He is spotless, because He is accepted, God is not examining me. He has examined the Lamb and accepted me on the basis of that Lamb. There is nothing that I have done in Adam that is more powerful than what God did in Christ!

A careful study of the whole chapter of Hebrews 10 will confirm much of this for us. One of the things that it declares is that the sacrifices that were offered there year by year could not make the worshipers perfect concerning conscience. If it could have they would have ceased to have been offered. In those sacrifices there is a remembrance again made of sins every year because it is impossible for the blood of bulls and goats to take away sin. When Jesus came into the world He said that sacrifice and offering is not what you are looking for, but you have prepared for me a body. In other words, Jesus would become the ultimate sacrifice that would not only cover the sin of the world; it would take away the sin of the world. Perfection would no longer be based on performing the laws of an old covenant. Our perfection would be based upon the sacrifice of Jesus Christ.

> *"For the law having a shadow of good things to come, and not*
> *the very image of the things, can never with those sacrifices*

which they offered year by year continually make the comers thereunto perfect. For then would they not have ceased to be offered? because that the worshippers once purged should have had no more conscience of sins." (Heb. 10:1-2 KJV)

I am not sure that we have ever fully grasped the power of Hebrews 10, especially verse 2 that says, "For then would they not have ceased to be offered." Because that the worshippers once purged should have had no more conscience of sins. In other words, a true revelation of the sacrifice of Jesus Christ will remove the sin consciousness. Can you see that this man, who was born blind, is really trapped into a system that constantly points out your sin? In the new covenant we should have no more consciousness of sin, but that is what we preach over American pulpits every week. It is because we do not fully understand that the work of the sacrifice of Jesus Christ once and for all time took care of my sin; my past, present and future sin. You see, whenever I make a mistake and sin, it does not mean that the sacrifice has to be offered again. It means that we were already completely covered. You might say, "Well, Brother Hiles, you mean to tell me that my future sins have been taken care of?" The answer is yes, because all of your sins were in the future when Jesus died on the cross. He paid for them in advance. That does not mean that we should continue to sin. The apostle Paul would say how can we who are dead to sin live any longer in it?

He tells us in Hebrews 10:10, "By the which will we are sanctified through the offering of the body of Jesus Christ once for all." Our sanctification is not on the basis of our performance. It is on the basis of the offering of the body of Jesus Christ, once and for all. When you understand that your sanctification is on the basis of an offering, then you can stand and say with confidence, "I am, in fact, sanctified".

Verses 12-14 of the same chapter says, "But this man, after he had offered one sacrifice for sins forever, sat down on the right hand of God; From henceforth expecting till his enemies be made his footstool. For by one offering he hath perfected forever them that are sanctified." Do you remember that just a verse above this it tells us that we were sanctified by the offering of the body of Jesus Christ so that our sanctification and our perfection is not on the basis of our performance? It is on the basis of the sacrifice of Jesus Christ so that we should be able to stand in this day and say, "Not only have I been forgiven but I am sanctified and perfected because of the work of this sacrifice."

Someone might say, "What about Hebrews chapter 6? It says 'Therefore leaving the principles of the doctrine of Christ, let us go on unto perfection.'" What you will find in that chapter is that the word perfection in the Greek is not a verb, it is a noun. A verb is an action word which means it is something you do. The word perfection there is a noun and a noun is the name of a person, place or thing. When he is saying let us go on unto perfection, He is simply saying that we must go on into this perfect One, who is Christ. Once you are in Him your sanctification and your perfection is His because you are in Christ, the perfect One.

> *"But of him are ye in Christ Jesus, who of God is made unto us wisdom, and righteousness, and sanctification, and redemption: That, according as it is written, He that glorieth, let him glory in the Lord."* (I Cor. 1:30-31 KJV)

I think if we are ever able to renew our minds with this truth we will begin to walk out of that perfection that we already have. We are not trying to get to salvation; we are working out of salvation with fear and trembling.

WHAT A DISAPPOINTMENT

A powerful Old Testament picture of this is Rachel and Leah. Jacob goes down to find a wife for himself and he finds a man by the name of Laban. When he finds Laban, he has two daughters; one named Leah, whose name means "weary" and one named Rachel, whose name means "the ewe lamb".[1] Jacob falls in love with Rachel, or should I say, he falls in love with the lamb. He is passionately in love with the lamb and he goes to Laban and says, "What must I do in order to enter into covenant relationship with Rachel (the lamb)?" Laban says, "You have to work for me for seven long years and then at the end of your work I will give you her to be your wife". Isn't that much like the religious systems that most of us have sat under? We were told that when we fell in love with the Lamb that the only way you can get it is to work and labor, labor and work? We did it. We did all of those things as if it were just a day and we labored, thinking that one day we were going to get the Lamb. What we don't understand is that there was an older sister that, according to law, had to be married first.

You know the story. Laban tricks Jacob into marrying Leah. The great celebration and the wedding feast arrive and the veil is put over the face of Leah, as was the custom of that day. Isn't it amazing that the veil always speaks of the law in the New Testament?

> "But even unto this day, when Moses is read, the vail is upon their heart. Nevertheless when it shall turn to the Lord, the vail shall be taken away. Now the Lord is that Spirit: and where the Spirit of the Lord is, there is liberty. But we all, with open face beholding as in a glass the glory of the Lord, are changed into the same image from glory to glory, even as by the Spirit of the Lord." (2 Cor. 3:15-18 KJV)

When we go to receive, many times all we get is something that is veiled and we don't even know what we are getting. In reality we are really reaching and thinking we are going to get the lamb and all we get is Leah, or "weary". Have you come to that place? Remember the opening chapter of this in the Message Bible says, "Are you weary, tired and burned out on religion?" I think the answer to that is many of us have lifted the veil in the morning after the honeymoon of our new birth only to discover that religious Laban has married us to the wrong covenant. We woke up one morning and we were not in intimate relationship with the Lamb; we were in a covenant with the law and legalism and all we got was weary!

The King James Version describes Leah as being "tender eyed", while another translation says she had a "dumb look in her eyes". My brother-in-law describes her like this, "She has blue eyes; one blew north and one blew south." Many have started out their journey very blindly, very much like this man born blind. They have entered into a religious system and they really don't know what's under that veil, blind to what they are going to get. Can you imagine the startle that was in the eyes of Jacob as he woke up the morning after their wedding and he had already consummated this relationship, and it is everlastingly too late to take her back to Laban? He rolls over to kiss his bride good morning and instead of being in bed with the lamb and in bed with Rachel, he is in bed with weary Leah who has a wild look in her eye. Can you imagine the disappointment that was in his heart as he would come out of that bedchamber, headed for Laban's house to say, "You have tricked me? I've been bamboozled. I have been lied to and I've been hoodwinked." I think that is the response that is coming to many who are now waking up to the message of grace.

It is interesting to note that Leah's name also means "a wild cow".[2] I think many are waking up in this hour realizing that, "While I thought I was reaching for the Lamb, all I got was weary. I woke up with a wild cow with a dumb look in its eyes and I am now very angry that I have been tricked by a religious system that did not produce for me what I thought I was going to get".

Jacob goes up to the house of Laban and says, "You promised me that I could have Rachel to wed." Laban says to him, "Yes, but the law says that the oldest has to marry first." Isn't it amazing that we always have to quote the law and the law was the first covenant, so to speak, and we were bound to that first covenant? Here's the good news. Laban says to him, "I tell you what I am going to do. You fulfill the week, which belongs to Leah." I think we can literally see that Jesus fulfilled that week, so to speak. He fulfilled the law of the Mosaic system and He fulfilled all of the obligations that we had to that system of being weary; that system of a wild cow and that system that has a dumb look in its eyes. He fulfilled all of that so that He could come back and give us Rachel, the Lamb, to be in covenant with. Laban says to him, "I am going to give her to you at the beginning of this and then you can work for me for another seven years". You say, "What does that mean, Brother Hiles?" What I would simply say is that you cannot work to get this, but once you get it, you will work. In other words, he worked seven years and got weary. But what happened is he was disappointed with that. Now we simply receive, as the free gift, this Lamb and we work out of salvation with fear and trembling.

> *"This is the covenant that I will make with them after those days, saith God, I will put my laws into the hearts and into their minds will I write them and their sins and iniquities I will remember no more. Now where remission of these is, there is no more offering for sin. Having therefore, brethren, boldness to enter into the holiest by the blood of Jesus by a new and living way, which he hath consecrated for us, through the veil, that is to say, his flesh."* (Hebrews 10:16-21 KJV)

This new covenant is not one that points out who sinned, as was the case in John 9. This is the answer that Jesus gave to them when they asked Him who sinned.

> *"Jesus answered, Neither hath this man sinned, nor his parents: but that the works of God should be made manifest in him. I must work the works of him that sent me, while it is day: the night cometh, when no man can work."* (John 9:3-4 KJV)

I think what Jesus is describing in these verses is not simply that He is about to do a miracle, but that the works that God gave Him to do was the work of the cross and the work of redemption to humanity, and the work of removing sin to bring us into a new covenant.

The New Creation is Human and Divine

What Jesus does then is spit on the ground and mixes His spittle to make clay. He anoints the eyes of the blind man with the clay and then He tells him to go wash in the pool of Siloam, which is by interpretation called "sent". When I think of this powerful symbolism, what I'm seeing is that he is mixing the clay of the realm of Adam's dust with the spittle of the divine DNA of the Son of God. The human and the divine are about to come together again, much like it did in the day God would create man. He would bring together the red clay of earth and then He would breathe into it the divine life of God and cause the first man Adam to be human and divine. He would give access to both the visible and invisible realms, the heavens and the earth, the natural and spiritual. One more time, God is about to connect the interface of the human and the divine. The human and divine are about to come together. You see, the new creation is not simply divine, but human and divine. It is a divine compound of the best of both worlds.

On the morning of the 6th day God creates man, in the presence of angels who are giving Him glory. I think Michael probably looked over at Gabriel and said, "He outdid Himself yesterday in creation. I wonder what He is going to make today." About that split second in time God leans back and says, "Let's make a man in our image and after our likeness and let him have dominion." Then all of a sudden angels began to declare, "We're about to see what God would look like if He were visible." In that split second of time God descends from the heavens and takes a lump of red clay and like the hand of a great potter He begins to shape His image and likeness into that lump of clay. He might have done it like a snow angel. He may have just made a divine impression so that the image of the invisible God was about to become visible. But as He shaped and molded Himself into that lump of red clay, I can hear the angels say, "He is out of the earth. And because He is out of the earth, He is earthy." But at that split second in time, God ascends into the deepest depths of spirit substance into the heavens itself, and He fills his lungs full of a breath of spirit essence. When He comes down on Adam He gives him mouth-to-mouth resuscitation and breathes into him the breath of life, and the human and divine merge. The interface between heaven and earth, the human and the divine, the visible and the invisible, have now come together in the person of a man.

In the fall of Adam a disconnect was made between the human and the divine. Before that, Adam had access to the visible and the invisible. I believe that he could not only name the animals, but he knew angels by their names. He walked and talked with God in the cool of the day. What God desired to do, even in the redemptive work of Christ, was bring man back into that place; because once man disconnected that interface and separated himself, he simply became earthy. I think that when Jesus comes on the scene 4,000 years later, when God leans over the balconies of glory and sees Mary bowed in pain to give birth to the firstborn son of the living God, the human and the divine had once more come together. He was very God and very man. He was human and divine. The interface between God and man had now been reconnected in a man. The heavens which had been like brass were now about to be open and access given to the human family to come back into relationship with the living God who was now their Father. God and man could once again communicate in the cool or spirit of the day. Perhaps this scripture is confirming this thought.

> *"That in the dispensation of the fulness of times he might gather together in one all things in Christ, both which are in heaven, and which are on earth; even in him:"* (Eph 1:10 KJV)

King Solomon gets a hold of that in the Song of Solomon and writes, "My beloved is white and ruddy." In other words, white the divine and red of Adam, because when God mixes the two, He has the human and the divine. You see, when we are born from above as the new creation man, God reconnects the interface of spirit substance into our lives. He interfaces the human and the divine. When He is putting this spittle and this clay in the man's eyes I think he is restoring his vision to what he was in the original creation. He is trying to bring him back to who he was in the original creation before the fall.

To be human does not mean you are Adamic or you are in the old creation. When the human merges with the divine, the Spirit of the living God comes into us and that divine connection is made. Then we have the best of both worlds where once again we have access to the invisible and the visible to the heavens and the earth. I think so much so that when you look at the original creation of Adam in the garden, you cannot tell if this man is in a garden or is the garden in this man, or is it both? The answer is probably both. Just because you are a new creature does not mean that you don't have feelings. I have heard people say, "I am a dead man walking", but that it is not really true. You are not a dead man walking. You are a new creation; a living being that is human and divine. You still have emotions and you still have desires. You still bleed when people cut you. You are still hurt when they say all manner of evil against you. It is just that you have chosen now not to live out of your carnal nature. You have chosen to live out of your divine nature of which you are a partaker. You simply reconnected yourself to the tree of life. You have discovered that living from the tree of knowledge of good and evil only makes you weary. You discovered that you cannot do this on your own. You cannot get enough information about good and evil to make yourself like God. You cannot live the Christian life. It is then that you turn to this life source and reconnect yourself to the divine life that lives inside of you. Your utter dependence is upon the one who lives within you to live this life through you.

AN APOSTOLIC POOL

I think it is incredible that Jesus sends this man to a pool called Siloam, which is by interpretation "sent". This word "sent" comes from Strong's Concordance #649 and is the Greek word apostelo. It means to send out. It means "to send out properly on a mission", literally or figuratively. It means to send away, to send forth out or to set at liberty. The root word for the word apostle in the New Testament is this very word. When Jesus is sending this man to a pool called Siloam to get his vision corrected, He sends him literally to an apostolic pool. That is what is being pictured here.

As I have written in other chapters, I believe there is a new kind of apostle on the scene that will not bring you back to your sin consciousness or who you were in Adam. It will bring you to a place of washing where you can be sent away in a state of liberty, no longer with a sin consciousness of who sinned, this man or his parents.

Tragically enough, I think misguided apostles have brought people to this apostolic pool and instead of sending them away seeing and sending them away so that they depart in a state of liberty, they have put them under more bondage than the people had before they came.

> *"How then shall they call on him in whom they have not believed? and how shall they believe in him of whom they have not heard? and how shall they hear without a preacher? And how shall they preach, except they be sent? as it is written, How beautiful are the feet of them that preach the gospel of peace, and bring glad tidings of good things!"* (Rom. 10:14-15 KJV)

This declares how shall they preach except they be sent. This word "sent" is the same Greek word as Strong's #649. It again denotes the same idea that this pool they are coming to is an apostolic pool. In this very text He said, "How beautiful are the feet of them that preach the gospel of peace and bring glad tidings of good things." You see, the gospel is the good news. It is the teaching of the death, burial and resurrection of Jesus Christ. It literally brings the glad tidings.

He further says in verse 17, "So then faith cometh by hearing, and hearing by the word of God." The thing I would point out here is that if you look up the word "God" in the interlinear Bible, it is not the Greek word for God. It is the Greek word for Christ. It literally reads, "So then faith cometh by hearing and hearing by the word of Christ." When we preach Christ it brings people to an apostolic pool that opens their eyes, not to their sin consciousness, but to who they are in this new creation man.

It is also interesting to note that in the book of Nehemiah this pool of Siloam is called the king's fountain, or the gate of the fountain, or the king's pool.

"So I came to Jerusalem, and was there three days. And I arose in the night, I and some few men with me; neither told I any man what my God had put in my heart to do at Jerusalem: neither was there any beast with me, save the beast that I rode upon. And I went out by night by the gate of the valley, even before the dragon well, and to the dung port, and viewed the walls of Jerusalem, which were broken down, and the gates thereof were consumed with fire. Then I went on to the gate of the fountain, and to the king's pool: but there was no place for the beast that was under me to pass." (Neh. 2:11-14 KJV)

Nehemiah has come into the city of Jerusalem and is there literally for three days. Now anytime I see the terminology three days in the scripture, I am always reminded of the three days and three nights of the person and work of Jesus Christ. Nehemiah is coming into Jerusalem to assess the condition of the city in the night season. He discovers the walls are broken down and burned with fire. They are in Babylonian captivity. This is a powerful picture of the church in the beginning stages of restoration. They have been under Babylonian religious confusion that has kept people blind to the person and work of Jesus Christ. Please note that in this scripture one of the reasons they are in Babylonian captivity is because they did not keep Sabbath.

And them that had escaped from the sword carried he away to Babylon; where they were servants to him and his sons until the reign of the kingdom of Persia:

To fulfil the word of the Lord by the mouth of Jeremiah, until the land had enjoyed her sabbaths: for as long as she lay desolate she kept sabbath, to fulfil threescore and ten years. (2 Chron. 36:20-21 KJV)

A man by the name of Nehemiah comes into the city in the night to assess this situation and the condition of the city, or the church, in the night season. Note that Nehemiah's name means "the comforter", so he is a type of the Holy Spirit. In Nehemiah 1:1 he comes in a month called Chisleu. The word Chisleu means "hope". He comes in the 20th year which is the number for redemption, and he comes into the palace Shushan. Shushan literally means "the lily palace". A lily is the symbol of resurrection. There was one person with him that I think is important to notice and that is Hanani. Hanani's name means "grace". Let me just sum this up. We have a man called "the comforter" coming in a month called "hope" in the year of "redemption" in "resurrection" palace with a man by the name of "grace". Ultimately Hanani becomes the governor of the city. In other words, grace begins to reign and rule. I think that is the whole purpose of the new covenant. Because of the abundance of grace and the gift of righteousness, we reign in life by one Christ Jesus. So grace has to become the governor of our lives.

Nehemiah comes into this city to survey the condition of the city. He says that there was "no beast with me save the beast that I rode in on."

> *"I went out by night by the gate of the valley, even before the dragon well, and to the dung port, and viewed the walls of Jerusalem, which were broken down, and the gates thereof were consumed with fire. Then I went on to the gate of the fountain, and to the king's pool: but there was no place for the beast that was under me to pass."* (Neh. 2:13-14 KJV)

This is incredibly interesting because the first place he stops is at a dragon well and a dung port. In other words, if you are going to be part of this great reformation and this gospel revolution, you are going to have to see the condition of the city, or the church, in the night season. When he rides into the city, he rides in with a beast underneath him and he comes into the valley gate before the dragon well. One of the first things to notice here is that the reason this was called the dragon well was because legend has it that it was where the head of a dragon was cut off. Therefore, the first step of restoration to the church is that we must tell the people that the devil has been defeated and that Jesus has spoiled principalities and powers.

It is amazing to me that many places that you go there is more emphasis on the devil and what the devil is doing than there is on God and what God is doing. Many places you go the people couldn't have church without the devil. They could not receive an offering without threatening you with the devil. We give in offerings to make the devil mad rather than giving to God because we are in love with him. They say things like, "I know we are going to have a good service because the devil was really fighting me today." In other words, we give way too much place to the devil. I am not saying that I do not believe in a devil. I just believe that he is really defeated and that we have the victory over him.

I don't want to dwell too much on that, but I do want to take a look at this word dragon. It is also a word that can be translated as "a jackal" or "dog". That connects me to my next thought about this king's pool and fountain gate to which we are about to come. This gate at the fountain and this king's pool is the same gate called "the pool of Siloam" in the new covenant. Before we can come to that, we have to first pass by and settle some things concerning this dragon well and dung port. When I saw that the word for "dragon" could also be translated as "jackals" or "dogs" my mind immediately went to the apostle Paul's words in Philippians 3:2 where he says, "Beware of dogs, beware of evil workers, and beware of the concision." Now I don't think that Paul was simply saying "beware of dogs that bark in the yard". He is identifying this word "dogs" with these evil workers; or these people who are part of the cutting group of concision, the Judaizers. Paul was dealing with those who wanted to bring a mixture of law and grace and pollute this pool of Siloam. He goes on to say:

> *"For we are the circumcision, which worship God in the spirit, and rejoice in Christ Jesus, and have no confidence in the flesh. Though I might also have confidence in the flesh. If any other man thinketh that he hath whereof he might trust in the flesh, I more: Circumcised the eighth day, of the stock of Israel, of the tribe of Benjamin, an Hebrew of the Hebrews; as touching the law, a Pharisee; Concerning zeal, persecuting the church;*

touching the righteousness which is in the law, blameless. But what things were gain to me, those I counted loss for Christ. Yea doubtless, and I count all things but loss for the excellency of the knowledge of Christ Jesus my Lord: for whom I have suffered the loss of all things, and do count them but dung, that I may win Christ, And be found in him, not having mine own righteousness, which is of the law, but that which is through the faith of Christ, the righteousness which is of God by faith: That I may know him, and the power of his resurrection, and the fellowship of his sufferings, being made conformable unto his death." (Phil. 3:3-10 KJV)

We have already addressed this scripture in some other chapters of this book but one of the things that I want to point out to you is that the apostle Paul begins to give his credentials. He begins to tell them that he was circumcised the eighth day and was out of the tribe of Benjamin. He persecuted the church, as touching the righteousness, which is of the law. He was absolutely blameless. But what Paul ultimately goes on to say is he was once a part of this cutting group, this concision. That was when Paul said to them, "Yeah doubtless, I count all things but loss for the excellency of the knowledge of Christ Jesus my Lord, for whom I have suffered the loss of all things and do count them but dung, that I might win Christ." In other words, Paul says that he counts all of that religious garbage that he came up under as dung. Thus, it brings us to the whole concept of Nehemiah, who has not only come to the dragon well and discovered the head of the dragon has been cut off, but he has also realized that you cannot drink from the well of Judaism or religion or from the "jackals" or dogs of the concision if you're going to be part of a restoration. He next comes to the dung port because if you are going to come into restoration, you are going to have to get rid of the dung of self-righteousness that comes from performance-based religion. Paul counted all of his religious background as dung that he might win Christ.

You see when he came to the dung port it was ultimately outhouse row. It was God showing Nehemiah how to get rid of all of the byproducts of his flesh. In other words, before we come to the king's pool or the pool of Siloam, we must learn how to get rid of our religious dung.

Let's take a look at how God did that in the book of Deuteronomy with the children of Israel when they were in the wilderness journey.

Let's Get the Dung Out of the Camp

"If there be among you any man, that is not clean by reason of uncleanness that chanceth him by night, then shall he go abroad out of the camp, he shall not come within the camp: But it shall be, when evening cometh on, he shall wash himself with water: and when the sun is down, he shall come into the camp again. Thou shalt have a place also without the camp, whither thou shalt go forth abroad: And thou shalt have a paddle upon thy weapon; and it shall be, when thou wilt ease thyself abroad, thou shalt dig therewith, and shalt turn back and cover that which cometh from thee: For the LORD thy God walketh in the midst of thy camp, to deliver thee, and to give up thine enemies before thee; therefore shall thy camp be holy: that he see no unclean thing in thee, and turn away from thee." (Deut. 23:10-14 KJV)

Can you imagine coming through the wilderness journey as Moses did leading three to six million people? I don't know if you've ever thought about it or not, but it had to be a logistical nightmare. If he had three to six million people, no wonder it took them 40 years. Because if there was no rest area, how many times do you think that they had to stop and go to the bathroom? Maybe you think that's not important, but God thought it important enough to write it in the scripture in this text. He told them that if there is any man unclean by reason of that which chances him by night that he should go forth outside of the camp and come not within the camp. If he should get any, if I can call it "religious dung", on him then he would need to wash himself with water and wait until the sun goes down so that he can come back into the camp. The Lord told them to go forth outside of the camp so that when he walked among them there would be no uncleanness. In verse 14 he says, "For the Lord thy God walks in the midst of the camp to deliver thee to give up thine enemies before thee, therefore shall thy camp be Holy that he see no unclean thing in thee and turn away from thee." You see, God will come in the midst of the camp to destroy our enemies from before our faces, if he comes in the camp and finds no uncleanness. Therefore, there must be a place outside the camp where we can get rid of our uncleanness. He issues to every man what King James calls "a paddle upon thy weapon." I like how King James says it in verse 13, "And thou shall have a paddle upon thy weapon and it shall be when thou wilt ease thyself abroad, thou shall dig therewith and shall turn back and cover that which cometh of thee." In other words, he issued to every man, as standard equipment, a paddle, literally a shovel or a port-a-potty if you will, that he would carry on his belt so that when he had to go to the bathroom he could literally go outside of the camp and dig a whole and cover that which came forth from him.

I think it is interesting that this word paddle is from the Hebrew #3489 in Strong's concordance and it is translated as a "nail, paddle, pin or a stake". You ask, "How is that relevant to this message Brother Hiles?" It is because what was occurring here was that he was showing them how Jesus got rid of all of our religious dung, as well as our by-products of our flesh on any level.

> *"For the bodies of those beasts, whose blood is brought into the sanctuary by the high priest for sin, are burned without the camp. Wherefore Jesus also, that he might sanctify the people with his own blood, suffered without the gate. Let us go forth therefore unto him without the camp, bearing his reproach."*
> (Heb. 13:11-13 KJV)

This tells you that outside of the camp Jesus suffered without the gate and what was occurring was, Jesus took a nail and with that nail He took all of the handwriting of ordinance that was against us. He took the nail and got rid of all of our religious dung. He got rid of all of the by-products of our flesh and all of the refuse and all of our stink and mess that comes out of us. He took it outside of the camp, nailed it to the cross, dug a hole and buried it in the tomb of Joseph of Arimathea. He is asking us to go forth outside of the camp, unto Him without the camp bearing His reproach. It is at that place He washes us with pure water. He cleanses us that we can come back into the camp clean so that the Lord God can walk among us and defeat all of our enemies.

I believe that is what is occurring here as far as what this man born blind coming to the pool of Siloam pictures. It pictures us coming to an apostolic pool that will show us how Jesus took all of our religious dung, all of our fleshly dung, our entire stink, and took it outside of the camp and got rid of it with a nail. This man was born blind but by the time he walks through this process and comes to the pool of Siloam, he is coming to a different kind of pool that can open his eyes.

I think it is incredible to note that when Nehemiah comes into this city and after he passes by the dragon well and passes the dung port, he sees that the first step of restoration is that he is going to have to deal with the dragon, deal with these dogs of religion, deal with getting rid of all of the dung. Then, all of a sudden he comes to the gate of the fountain, to the king's pool, which in the New Testament is called the pool of Siloam. When he gets there he makes this statement, "There was no place for the beast that was under me to pass." I don't think he is simply talking about the donkey on which he rode. Of course, that is certainly what he probably did, but something more powerful is being pictured here. You see, while many are worried about some beast to come in the book of Revelation, I think the one he is dealing with is the one we rode in on called "our old nature".

I like how the Amplified Bible says in Colossians 3:5, "So kill (deaden, deprive of power) the evil desire lurking in your members [those animal impulses and all that is earthly in you that is employed in sin]" and he describes what they are as "sexual vice, impurity, sensual appetites, unholy desires, and all greed and covetousness, for that is idolatry (the deifying of self and other created things instead of God)." What you see is that the beast he is dealing with is not one in the White House nor is he the one across the sea somewhere in the Middle East. It is the beast of man's fallen state with which we must part company. While I have already taught you that Adam is dead and he is not dying; you must also realize that Nehemiah was surveying the condition of the city in the night season. The night season is when you don't have any revelation. Until you pass by the dragon well and the dung port and get a revelation of what took place outside the camp in the death and burial of Jesus Christ, you will continue to ride your beast. You will live in the lie of who you are in Adam and remain in your night season. But when you come to the King's Fountain, the pool of Siloam, and your eyes are opened, it will be from this position that you can kill, deaden and deprive the animal impulses that are lurking in your members. They are not in your nature. They are in your members, and one of the most unruly members that must be tamed is our tongue.

You see, once you see how Jesus dealt with your dung and your dogs and your old nature, you will come to a place where you can no longer live out of these evil desires.

> *"In view of the fact, therefore, that you were raised with Christ, the things above be constantly seeking, where Christ is, on the right hand of God, seated. The things above be constantly setting your mind upon, not the things on the earth; for you died, and your life has been hidden with Christ in God. Whenever the Christ is made visible, our life, then also you with Him shall be manifested in glory."* (Col. 3:1 WUEST)

In other words, since you are a new creature do not allow these animal impulses to lurk in your members any longer. You see, it's really not the beast in the White House or the beast in any other house that bothers me. It is the beast that we allow to live in our house. I am telling you that in this day of restoration we have come to a pool of Siloam. We have come to an apostolic pool and there is no place for the beast that is under us to pass. We must part company with our beast.

Where There is No Vision

Now let's address the vision of this man as Jesus restores his eyesight. First of all, I just want to say that this man used to beg because he was blind. This is what happens to us when we are under the religious bondage that keeps us blind to who we are in Christ. Instead of making us know who we are, it makes us feel like we need to come to God and beg Him for everything that we need, not knowing that we don't have to beg God. He is our Father and we are sons and we have a legal right to healing.

Many times we quote the scripture from Proverbs "where there is no vision the people perish". We fail to really understand that the vision he is talking about is really not dealing with a program or plan or some kind of a fund raising event or thermometer on the wall that we call our vision. It is from the Strong's concordance Old Testament word #2377. Chazown is an Old Testament word that means a dream, a revelation or an oracle. Literally what he is saying is that without a vision or revelation of Jesus Christ, without a prophetic vision or oracle, the people will perish.

The greatest need of a human family right now on the earth is that we need a vision of Jesus Christ. We need a revelation of His finished work. There is no need that we have or problem that we cannot solve with a revelation of Him. Let's take a look at this scripture:

> *"And the Lord answered me, and said, Write the vision, and make it plain upon tables, that he may run that readeth it. For the vision is yet for an appointed time, but at the end it shall speak, and not lie: though it tarry, wait for it; because it will surely come, it will not tarry."* (Hab. 2:2-3 KJV)

I want you to pay special attention that in the book of Habakkuk the vision is an "it" and it is "yet for an appointed time and at the time of the end it will speak and not lie, though it tarry, wait for it because it will surely come, it would not tarry." Over and over the word used is "it" in the Old Testament, but what I want you see is that if you compare that with the Hebrews 10:37-39 KJV, "For yet a little while, and he that shall come will come, and will not tarry. Now the just shall live by faith: but if any man draw back, my soul shall have no pleasure in him. But we are not of them who draw back unto perdition; but of them that believe to the saving of the soul."

Now the word "it" is changed to "he". It says "for yet a little while and he that shall come will come and will not tarry." In the new covenant the vision is no longer an "it". It is now a "He". In the new covenant what our eyes are being opened to is the work of Jesus Christ. They are being opened to the walk of faith. In the new covenant we are not living by works, we are living by faith and we are not drawing back. To draw back does not simply mean we are drawing back to going back to watching movies or something else that we have called sin. He is saying that we are not going to draw back unto perdition. Literally, we are not going to go back to the whole idea of the old covenant system that was full of death, judgment and damnation. But we are of them who believe to the saving of the soul. Compare that with this verse.

> "But that no man is justified by the law in the sight of God, it is evident: for, the just shall live by faith. And the law is not of faith: but, The man that doeth them shall live in them. Christ hath redeemed us from the curse of the law, being made a curse for us: for it is written, Cursed is every one that hangeth on a tree." (Gal. 3:11-13 KJV)

He goes on to quote directly from the book of Habakkuk and says that the just will live by faith. Remember what I have already written a few chapters before this? Faith comes by hearing and hearing by the word of Christ. When we hear the gospel, we hear the finished work of Christ. We begin to live out of what we believe to be true. In other words, if I believe that I am just, I am going to live like I am just. The clear point here is that in the book of Galatians the law is not of faith. It shuts up faith and keeps us blind to the revelation of who we are in Christ. As a result we perish for lack of vision and knowledge of Him. We continued to stumble around still struggling with the question of whose sin caused my problems, begging for a token of blessing. But when I see Him, my vision becomes clearer. Scales fall from my eyes and I realize that He has already paid in full for my sins and the sins of my parents. I have been redeemed from the curse of the law. I have come to an apostolic pool and now my vision is clear. Real apostles will preach Christ and they will point you to Him and not to themselves.

I think it is incredible to note that Habakkuk said, "In the end it will speak." What that says to me is that the end was not just somewhere out in our distant future but it was the end of the age of the law that had now come to a conclusion. For in the end the vision would become a "He" and "He" would speak and "He" is now on the scene speaking.

Hebrews 9 says, "Once in the end of the world, hath he appeared to put away sin by the sacrifice of himself." That is not something He is going to do. That is something He already did. He came at the end of the world. The word "world" here is translated in other translations as "age". He is not talking about the end of a global situation. He is talking about the end of the covenant of the law, and what he is showing you in this new covenant we don't walk by an "it" but we walk by faith. Compare that with Romans 1:16-17. In these verses he tells us that we should not be ashamed of the gospel of Christ because the gospel is defined as the death, burial and resurrection of Jesus Christ, or if you will, the finished work. It is the power of God unto salvation because when you preach the gospel of Christ, therein is the righteousness of God revealed from faith to faith. Once again he connects this to Habakkuk when he quotes the later part and says, "It is written that the just will live by faith." This is a direct connection to the book of Habakkuk.

Yes, I believe that the eyes of the blind are being opened at this pool called Siloam. I believe we are being sent to an apostolic pool, to a king's fountain, to a place that our eyes are opened to the gospel. Much like the apostle Paul, we have been knocked to the ground many times by our religious system, but we are receiving a touch that will open our eyes. I believe that through this book God will touch the eyes of apostles who are well-meaning men much like Paul, who are persecuting the church rather than edifying it. Many have already been knocked to the ground and found they are blind. They are blind much like Paul for three days. They do not have a revelation of the three days and three nights of the person work of Jesus Christ. Oh, but wait, God is sending an Ananias whose name means "grace". Because when the grace of God touches your eyes the scales will fall away just like they did this man who was at the pool of Siloam. You will become an apostle of grace. You will become a pool where others can wash their eyes and come away seeing. Perhaps we should be like the church of Ephesus in the book of Revelation. We should anoint our eyes with eye salve that we might see. I believe what is occurring here is Jesus is anointing his eyes with the eye salve that is being mixed with the clay, and the spit that will bring them back to a revelation of who they were in the original creation.

In the end the vision becomes a "He". It may have been an "it" in Habakkuk but in the book of Hebrews the "it" becomes a "He". That "He" is now standing in front of this blind man and He is saying to him, "You no longer have to remain in this condition of sitting here begging every week. You don't have to live in sin consciousness."

Isn't it amazing when Jesus would heal another man that was crippled He would say to him, "Son, thy sin be forgiven thee." The carnal mind of the Pharisees would go out of the safety zone and say, "Who does this man think He is to say to this man, 'Thy sin be forgiven thee'?" Jesus responds to them by saying, "Which is easier to say? Thy sin be forgiven thee, arise, take up thy bed and walk." I used to think, "Well, what in the world does 'thy sin be forgiven thee' have to do with this man being healed?" The Lord began to reveal to me that it is just as easy to say, "Thy sin be forgiven thee" as it is to say, "Rise, take up your bed and walk." Both are included in the atoning work of Jesus Christ, both healing and forgiveness of sin.

I believe that when He says to the man, "Thy sin be forgiven thee" that he is setting him up for a miracle. I think one of the things that keep us from receiving the miraculous is sin-consciousness. We walk down a church aisle and the first thing that hits our mind is not faith, it is, "I wonder if I did something wrong? I wonder if there is sin in my life. I wonder if God can do this. I know He can but will He do it for me?" Then all of the doubt begins to flood in because we have been taught such sin-consciousness and it has caused us to be beggars.

> *"Is any sick among you? let him call for the elders of the church; and let them pray over him, anointing him with oil in the name of the Lord: And the prayer of faith shall save the sick, and the Lord shall raise him up; and if he have committed sins, they shall be forgiven him."* (James 5:14-15 KJV)

Right there in the middle of that great healing scripture James tells us if he has committed any sin that even his sin can't stop God from healing him.

You say, "Well, Brother Hiles, you mean God will heal sinners?" My response is that everybody that Jesus healed was a sinner. There was nobody saved at this particular point and Jesus was demonstrating the Kingdom of God and the new covenant that was about to come on the scene.

I believe that when we come to this pool it washes our eyes away from sin-consciousness. When I pondered this, I thought of the scripture where Jesus talked about whosoever sin you remit are remitted, and whosoever sin you retain are retained. I don't think that simply means we go around telling people, "I forgive your sin." But I do think every time we get in the pulpit we either have the power in the preaching to retain people's sin to them and cause them to leave there with sin-consciousness; or we have the power to preach the forgiveness of sin through the gospel so that men can come away from this apostolic pool being restored in their sight.

Isn't it amazing in this text in John 9 that not only do they accuse this man of being a sinner, but they accuse Jesus of being a sinner? Oh, don't get me wrong. I don't believe that we should preach a message that encourages people to sin. But I believe that preaching against sin is not how you get people to get free from sin. I believe that when the Holy Spirit comes, as I have written in prior chapters, He convinces you of righteousness. Once you really see that you are righteous, and you are just, then the just will live by faith. In other words, if you believe you are righteous, you will act like you are righteous, because right believing will produce right living.

Oh dear ones, I believe we are in the throes of a gospel revolution. I believe like Nehemiah we have come into the city in the night season. We have gone outside the camp to the place where the dung port was the place where God got rid of all of your dung. Now you see the dragon well, the place where the head of the dragon was cut off and the devil was defeated. Not only was the devil defeated, but the jackals were destroyed and all of the religious dogs of the concision have been dealt with. It is then that we will bring people to an apostolic pool that will open their eyes. The eyes of their understanding will be flooded with light so that they can know what the hope of their calling is, and what are the riches of glory of his inheritance is in the saints. This is the work of the comforter the Holy Spirit which is typified by Nehemiah's night ride.

We will come to a place where we realize the vision is no longer an "it" but a "He" and that when we see Him, we will be like John in the book of Revelation. We will fall down at His feet like a dead man and then He will lay this hand of five-fold ministry. His restored hand on our head will raise us up with the power of resurrection.

It might get you thrown out of the Synagogue alright, but you are in good company. I trust that by this portion of the book that your eyes have been opened and that you aren't standing in the background wondering, "Do I know who Jesus is?" I hope that there is a greater revelation of Him in your life. I would like to conclude with a few more remarks.

In John 9:35 Jesus heard that they had cast the man out of the Synagogue and when He found him He said to him, "Do you believe on the Son of God?" Then he said, "Who is he Lord that I might believe on him?" Jesus said unto him, "Thou has both seen him and it is He that talks with thee." The man said, "Lord, I believe and he worshipped Him." I believe that as we come to the conclusion of this book that would be the question that He would ask you, "Do you believe?" Because the only requirement of the new covenant is that you believe. Everything else flows out of what you believe. Right believing will produce right living. I hope that by now your answer is, Lord I believe!

He spoke to this man and said, "Thou hast both seen Him and it is He that talketh with thee." Can you just understand today that the Lord is both talking with you and you are now seeing Him? What should be occurring in your life is that worship should be erupting from not only your lips but from your life as you walk pleasing to God.

You have come into a perpetual Sabbath day. Honor that Sabbath day to keep it holy. Don't violate it by thinking you have to do all over again what Jesus has already done. You have come into the absolute unforced rhythm of grace.

Endnotes

1. J.B. Jackson, *A Dictionary of Scripture Proper Names,* 3rd edition (Loizeaux Brothers, Neptune, NJ. 1957) Pg. 57 & 58.

2. Wick Broomall, A.M. Th.M, *The Open Bible Biblical Cyclopedic Index* , (Thomas Nelson Publishers, Nashville,TN. 1975) Pg. 181.

Contact Us

LYNN HILES MINISTRIES
P.O. Box 127
Great Cacapon, WV 25422

Phone: 304-579-5336
eMail: info@lynnhiles.com
Web: www.lynnhiles.com

This book and all other books and materials
by Dr. Lynn Hiles are available at
www.lynnhiles.com or by phone at 304-579-5336.